Schools Of Thought

By

Robert Earl Kenney

First published by AuthorHouse 04/30/04

ISBN: 1-4184-6139-3 (e-book)
ISBN: 1-4184-3001-3 (Paperback)

Library of Congress Control Number: 2004091424

Printed in the United States of America
Bloomington, IN

This book is printed on acid free paper.

Dedicated to all the Sunshine's in the World.

"The unexamined life is not worth living." Socrates, quoted in Plato's *Apology*

"Something else an academic education will do for you. If you go along with it any considerable distance, it'll begin to give you an idea what size mind you have. What it'll fit and, maybe, what it won't. After a while, you'll have an idea what kind of thoughts your particular size mind should be wearing. For one thing, it may save you an extraordinary amount of time trying on ideas that don't suit you, aren't becoming to you. You'll begin to know your true measurements and dress your mind accordingly."

Mr. Antolini to Holden Caulfield in, 'The Catcher in the Rye'.

The turtle was upended in the middle of the highway, I couldnt't help but stop. Fancy, still passed out in the back seat, wouldn't care. I pulled over. The graveled fringe wouldn't let me stop quickly but I couldn't let that turtle, legs waving and neck stretching, remain stranded in the midst of a busy highway. Sliding to a stop, I quickly assessed the oncoming trafffic in the sideview. A tanker roared by, the pressure first pushing me back and then sucking me forward through the window. Two more cars passed and I saw a gap. I quickly opened the door slamming it behind me and darted out to the center line. The turtle was thirty yards ahead. I ran towards it scanning the oncoming traffic. It was still wobbling clockwise when I bent to pick it up. I stood there, turtle in hand, bottom up, legs pawing, head turned towards me as the next wave of vehicles rushed by. Fearfully judging my chances I gauged the distance of the truck ahead and dived towards the fringe, horn blowing angrily in my ear. Pausing for breath I looked down. The pawing legs, frenzied for a turtle, had slowed, but the head still bent, mouth working soundlessly, towards me. Bug eater I thought, grass muncher, try not to be crushed by humanity. I ventured deep into the woods, climbed down a ravine and placed his all fours at the beginning of deep grass thinking geography should keep him from making that mistake again. As it moved into cover I noticed it's shell had white spots on it. Seemed strange, I thought, as I turned back, turtles aren't normally that colorful. Contemplating turtles I failed to look back when I opened the car door and didn't see the extra wide coming. Something, a strap or chain, not secured properly, gracefully tapped the back of my head in its passing.

***

Robert Earl Kenney

John Locke/tabula rasa (Blank Slate)....

Anthropology - n. The science of the origin, culture, and development of human beings. (The American Heritage Dictionary, Second College Edition)

AAGH. OOMPH. The sunshine. OOmph. What a night, wait, I feel a body here. Oh no I didn't. I did. I picked the only female in the house who could eat corn off the cob through a picket fence. Ahh like I've been picky. Get dressed buckerette I've a date with my stock broker. Sure, sure, I'll call you again. I might need a template of your face to make Gorilla cookies.

The library is open now. I better hop my happy ass before the derelicts get there. I hate waiting in line to use the computers but I'm too cheap to get the Internet on mine. I wonder if any new jobs have popped up. Four years of college studying Anthropology and look where its gotten me. Still unmotivated and listless.

But I don't regret the college experience. Even if it was a generation later. Though much was reinventing the wheel, much more stimulated introspection. Concepts of time and space, civilization and evolution, nurtured the younger mind of the older man. Even the tenured professors, reciting lessons from yellowed pages, exposed hidden knowledge that incited a process of understanding. An understanding that, with retrospection, cemented a truth. Each of us, with or without the benefit of higher knowledge are ' The eyes of the Universe'.

I suppose its cognitive dissonance. A life unreflective of the mind. Possibly more influential role models would have made a difference for me. Some one whom I could look up to. A personal hero I could have emulated. A real life presence could have given guidance. No book of past heroes, saints, or scholars would have the same impact than looking into the eyes of some one who's risen above and succeeded, climbed their own mountains, faced

1

their own demons, and dared the fates to challenge them again. Such people are rare, and rarer still, the common individual who lives a life in relative obscurity, recieve due accolades for lifes deeds and successes. A life lived above the common standards.

Well there appears to be no new jobs I'm interested in and I still have time to spare. I've tried before over the years, especially during college, just to see her name, but the various search engines have never turned her up. Let's try again. It has occurred to me that she might have gotten married. I hope so. She deserves the best.

I can't imagine that she would have missed out on the Information Age. Such a sparkling mind would have siezed upon this new technology and made it her own. Such a mind would not have been held back.

Well what is this? Some sort of organizational newsletter marketing a luncheon. It's a professional's luncheon. Something about expanding biodata outside the U.S.. It's dated November 1992 and there's a list of members in the back. They've all got titles, Associate Professors, PhD's, Directors of Management, Personnel Research, from both governmental and civilian sectors, and they all have one thing in common. They're Psychologists. And so is she, there's her name.

I have a hero, and her name is Sunshine.

Psychology - n. 1. The science of mental processes and behavior. 2. The emotional and behavioral characteristics, as of an individual or group. (The American Heritage Dictionary, Second College Edition)

***

Robert Earl Kenney

Rene Descartes/Cogito, ergo sum (I Think, Therefore I am)...

There are times when I read, I think of the mind that wrote the words. I know when I think, My thoughts are influenced by my past. And when I write, I have made judgements of a mindful past. Mindful in the sense that we have all made judgements of ourselves, the times in which we lived, from earliest understandings until the last memory, it is the most precious memories, good or bad, which define us. And memories, defined within the context of the times of our lives, require retrospection. When I read, I know I am thinking of the mind that wrote the words. And when I think, the words are colored by the thoughts of others. But my life is My life and I think, for so long as I can think, that is a good thing.

There's more to life I think, individually, than the antiseptic concept of babyhood, childhood, adolescence, adulthood, and old age. Without recognizing the variabilities of human experience, the natural binding of human minds, the natural hostility, the nurturing, the anger and hatred, the primal acculturated, there is no accounting suitable to know the minds of those past, present, and future. We are only human. And though it is understood there are stages in life for the sentient, it is up to the One to reflect upon his or hers continuum of life. To see ourselves in the mirror of the mind, to sense one's own stages, is to accept, not deny, the reality of one's present and why. And at some point it is clear why life is so precious. We remember. And in the annals of human conflict, the mind suffers.

I remember some things. I remember the first time I felt fear. I remember the first and second times I smoked a cigar. I remember the glorious year of my first love, and the second time I felt fear. I remember family and friends, the times good and bad. I remember military school, and subsequent career. I remember when I kissed Mom twice one morning and our last laugh, but I don't seem to be able to remember myself as I would have myself remembered or know myself now as I would remember myself to have been.

One of my earliest memories are of being in my mothers arms riding on the bus. I recall watching the telephone wires and how they connected to the poles and dipped in the middle and as the bus roamed down the street the wires seemed to bob and dip in perfect monotonous rythm. Mesmerizing. So was the destination.

The clinic was a red brick box with a huge plane glass window one could only see out of. It was full of people and the line was long. A huge woman with her youngin was right in front of us. Suddenly, she turned and barked at the youngin in her arms. I saw a bright yellow turd emerge on her ebony arm. She quickly disappeared down the corridor losing her place in line.

The nurse practiced quiet efficiency. Asking my mother questions and placing the responses on a clipboard. She stuck a stick in my mouth and bade me to say ΛΛH. Peered into some tube placed in my ears and nose, then beckoned the mother to take my pants down. She then produced a long needle from the counter. The mind thought,"What's that for?"....

My Mother was a beautiful human being. About 5'5", with an engaging sense of humor and personality. Brunette, and, when young, a looker. She taught me my ABC's and numbers. She nurtured and doted over me, and, I believe, provided me with the most loving and generous childhood she could. I have her sense of humor, her intelligence, and her alchoholism. She drank every day of my life.

She was born the youngest of three daughters to a rural couple in North Carolina. As a child she was very sickly and needed care over the years. Usually passed over to do the laundry and dishes or any other chores she became a spoiled and pretentious adult. After her father died, the girls went to live with their Aunt Nanny while their Mother found a job in the city. When this youngest daughter, my Mother, turned twenty one, she met the father of my two half brothers. He was 27, 6'3", semi-pro baseball player, and to her, dashing and elegant. After he was drafted, he volunteered to undergo medical experiments in order to stay out of the war. Those experiments left fistsized knots of muscle tissue on his arms and back. They married and had two boys. She never divorced him. He introduced her to alchohol, and started her into the abyss of addiction, this, coupled with a pretentious manner, caused the suffering of generations.

The early years might have been happy except for her increasing need to stay in bars. He was an uneducated man and also an alchoholic, despite good looks, and turned out to be a vicious woman and child beater. When the boys were 9 and 11, she ran away to California, leaving the children to a boys home. Due to this upbringing, the boys became morally corrupt and contributed to the criminal element of our society.

She landed a series of odd jobs, and managed to secure friends in times of need, "Gotta drink fella?". It was in a bar that she met my father. At 32, she gave birth to me in Alameda, California on November 15, 1954, around two in the morning. I was a surprise to both of them, not legally married, but he gave me his, and my, first name on this planet. It must have been raining that night, because a child named Robert surely screamed his way into this existence.

My Father was 27, a short man, 5'6", but heavily built due to his time in the Merchant Marines during the war, and subsequent enlistments in both the Army and Marines. He was adopted as a child by a Hawaiian woman who was friends with his mother, whom he never knew. His adoptive father was an old Cavalry Horse soldier who had been stationed in Hawaii. His lineage consisted of Hawaiian, Spanish, French, and Samoan. This along with the Irish, English of my Mother makes me the proverbial product of east meets west.

While Mom was an intelligent, witty woman with a high school education, Dad never finished the fifth grade. He has remained ignorant , embracing the more bizarre concepts of UFO"s, Governmental and World conspiracies, and the mysterious 12th planet.

Strangely enough, the first couple of years of my life are filled with the image of an old Hawaiian woman with bright shining eyes and a high squeaky voice. Forceful, wise, nurturing. She was my TU TU. My grandmother. The first years are considered the most formative. Where one establishes traits for a lifetime. For me, she was a guiding force, and I remember her fondly.

TuTu, the perpetuate of family and Hawaiian lore, spent many hours teaching Mom traditional dances and customs. It was TuTu who divined my future characteristics. Little ones have few things to distinguish themselves but I was fortunate. I had birthmarks on my left foot and the left side of my chin. Mom often repeated TuTu's predictions that I would have the gift of travel and the gift of speech.

The earliest years with my parents are hard to recall. But I remember the arguments. Even in the later years it was apparent she despised his ignorance and ineloquence, he her vanity and alchoholism. It was around Kindergarten that their union started to dissolve. I was in the back seat of the car waiting to go while they were in the house. A neighbor, whom they both knew, and who had been a close friend emerged from the house. He had just been talking to them and saw me in the car. He handed me a banana. They came out soon after.

"Where did he get the banana?" Him.

"You know where he got the banana."Her.

"Where did you get the banana?" Him to me.

Speechless. Me.

"I SAID, WHERE DID YOU GET THE BANANA?" Him.

"that guy" me.

"Didn't I tell you not to accept things from strangers?" Him furious.

He whirled and pounded me so hard that I remember the event to this day. They had been arguing again and he was in a jealous rage. I still see myself sitting there staring at the back of his head, knowing how wrong he was. Vowing not to forget how wrong he was. Ever.

***

I felt a touch, a sudden grasp to my right forearm, as of someone falling. I looked over. I was in a darkened room illuminated by a wall of light from an opened door. I was in a bed, a hospital bed. And a nurse, back framed by the light, was bent, briskly rubbing her left ankle. I heard her whisper, "damn." I blinked. Looking from her arm to her bent head I saw a pair of wings. Right at ther nape of her neck were light blue wings the size of two hands joined at the wrist, fringed with gold, the feathers pulsing with thin red veins, the red turning to pink and disappearing. She hopped forward on her one good foot and I returned her grasp as she raised up. A brown haired woman, eyes brightening then leveling with a matured gaze said gently," Welcome back."

The next morning an orderly, cautiously, entered my room. He said," Feel like some breakfast?" I nodded. He pushed a button on the side of the bed bringing me to a sitting position. He placed my breakfast on the side table and turned for the sliding L at the end of the room, maneuvering it chest high. As he placed my oatmeal and OJ in front of me I saw his wings. Bluish at the stems turning to light green feathers, tipped with red. I said, " Thanks. " He smiled a forced smile and bent towards the door. His wings fading from sight two steps before he exited to the hall. I knew something was different.

The Doctor entered soon after. We looked at each other as I sucked apple juice from the carton straw. Glancing down at my chart, eyes darting up from time to time, I heard him grunt in bewilderment. Then he said," How do you feel?" Standing at the foot of my bed I saw a starched white smock, fresh from the hanger, dutiful pen at the breast, light blue shirt collar and gray tie. A middle aged face thin, tight, and normally haggard, seemed flushed, cheeks reddened by an originality. I said," Okay.....what happened?" He said," You recieved an extreme blow to the back of the head.....You've been out for eight days now. Frankly you're an anomaly, such injuries ensure a slow comeback. I want you to relax, I'm gonna keep you for another day or two for observation. We'll contact your girlfriend for you..... I'm gonna prescribe some light sedatives. Please don't try to get up until I say so. Okay?" I nodded. He turned and began to write on my ledger. Looking over his shoulder I saw wings. Broad and strong, they waved slowly as he wrote. Luminous blue green with sad flecks of grey streaming to the tips. A cheery green pulsed through them as he turned and said," I'll see you tomorrow."

***

I boarded the bus crying. She told me everything would be all right. It was my first day and of course the future was mysterious. Kindergarten turned out to be pleasant with a lot of finger painting and posters. There seemed to be two rooms, one with chairs and one with mats for the afternoon nap.

I think the teacher liked me. One day all the mothers showed up for a group thing. We were all sitting in our chairs with the Mom's lining the wall and observing. At one point one of my classmates, during a singing thing, jumped up and sat on my lap. Always shy and still dreaming of girls with nebulous curiousity, I turned beet red. I saw the girls' Mother and mine sharing a laugh. I had big ears, curly hair and laughed freely. I had no thought of girls in other than not picking them for tag. Later that day, my Mom was to pick me up after all the others had gone. I was alone with my teacher. She asked me to come to her desk, picked me up and sat me on her lap. She held me close and talked to me. She was warm and I sensed her womanhood. Anxious and scared as she held me tightly, I pissed my pants.

It must have been soon after that Mom met Earl.

Earl Carl Dennis. A big handsome man, 6'3" about 230, with a beer belly and blond crewcut. An honest face that would light up when happy and be stern when not. I still love him. I remember the first time I saw him. My own Father had not been around for awhile. Mom brought him home with her. We were going to Chicago.

"Hi, what's your name?"

"Bobby."

"How old are you?"

"Five."

"How would you like to go on a trip?"

"Yeah, I'd like that....Mommy brought you for me, didn't she?"

Mom didn't tell me his past until I was in my twenties. He had spent time in jail for armed robbery. I knew he had been in the Korean War and been horribly burned from the waist down. Napalm. I never saw the scars unless he bent over. His own son, I saw a picture of him once, had died of leukemia at the age of 11. He got caught trying to pay the bills.

I still remember the trip. I plied him with questions. He answered with a common sense philosophy. He was kind, gentle, and a powerful figure for me. It was a glorious 5 days and nights watching cities, mountains, valleys, and towns pass by in the splendor of just being there. At night I would see the stars and wonder, see the lights of homes and wonder, to this day, who lives there. This trip was the transition from one Father to another.

I became Bobby Dennis.

***

A Review of Marco Polo's, <u>The Travels</u> (p.1-162)

Marco Polo's, <u>The Travels</u>, provide insight and knowledge of the mysterious, unknown lands to the east during a period in which the west struggled in its own identity. His collaboration in this writing, propitiously while a prisoner of war with the romance writer Rustichello (Intro p.17), details the cities, customs, cosmology, food, flora, fauna, and clothing of various peoples, not least of which the Mongols and their enigmatic leader Kubilai Khan.

Certainly, much of what is written is embellishment and folktale, oral histories passed down during his travels. Miracles, supporting the Christian faith, such as the Caliph of Baghdad's demand Christ's adherents move a mountain through faith, and the shoe-maker who made it so (p. 53-57), is a nod to the powers that be. The birth of the Mongol empire, their subservience to Prester John, and Chengis Khan's dismantling of his holdings (p. 93-96), serve the authors desire to lay the foundations of Kubilai Khan's greatness.

Still yet, viewing this tale of past societies with today's lense, we can discern much in the evolution of civilizations and innate beliefs, customs, and practices. Was the martyrdom of Mohametans in Tabriz, suffering death or injury at the hands of Christians, or, if looking at death and proclaiming Mohamet the messenger of God, they are saved (p. 57-58), a response to Pope Urban's plenary indulgence in 1095, initiating the Crusades? Does recent history, especially in regard to Iraq, reflect centuries old animosities?

Most fascinating is the breadth and scope of the Mongol Empire and their fierce yet benevolent ruler, Kubilai Khan. Merciless invaders, disciplined and skilled fighters, Polo describes their lifestyle, military organization, and cosmology (p.98) with astonishing clarity. In order to manage such a vast empire one must be able to command undying loyalty, have a magnetic personality, vision, and transcendent wisdom. Kubilai Khan's description as an average man belies this (p.122). His subsistence of the poor and religious (p.158), the banning of prostitution from the city (p.129), acceptance of Christianity without embracing it (p.119), and management of his dominion through a surprisingly efficient and sophisticated postal service (p.152-3), suggests both tolerance and enlightenment in contrast to a barbaric and savage reputation.

Work Cited

Polo, Marco. The Travels. Trans. Ronald Latham. England: Penguin, 1958.

∗∗∗

"The Doctor's said it didn't look good." Said Fancy. She seemed tense and her hand was sweaty. Francine Agnes Scrugood. She didn't like her last name, much less the other ones. Heavy set, thick silver framed glasses, she had spent much of her life proving herself in a man's world. But once you got through the tough exterior you found a warm and giving person if accepted into her ring. We had met in a pool tournament through a friend who thought she'd scare me and take me but I had tightened up and spanked her instead. We had become good friends, pool partners, and traveled together to various locales for advertised tournaments. I trusted her. She had proved a good friend. A very good friend.

Sensing I was strong enough she said," You little shit bird, what the hell happened? You weren't taking a leak were you?" I shook my head and told her about the turtle. She laughed and said," Well, I'm told I can take you home tomorrow, I'll tell Smith's you're among the living....... don't do that no more huh?" I smiled seeing her eyes watering up, grabbed her hand and kissed it. She pulled away first waving her hand at me then pointing her finger with kindness and turned to leave. I saw her wings quivering, a bluish brown, tipped with pink, pulsing with a gentle green and vanishing as she stepped into the hallway.

***

We settled in a small apartment on the southside of Chicago. He got a job as a truck driver and Mom assumed the role of domestic housewife. It was a beautiful thing to have two caring, nurturing adults in the same household. It was an old tenement building and we lived in the basement. I once watched a gang fight from the basement window. There was a fat Japanese kid who lived next door who became my playmate, we'd play wargames with our little plastic soldiers, he'd piss me off because he would never let me be the Americans. Often, my Daddy would take me to a Cubs game, the park, a drive, and the Zoo.

Going to the Zoo was a special event, and the prime attraction was the Monkey House. There was an old silverback gorilla who always had the largest audience and never failed to entertain. He lived in a 50' by 30' cage, concrete floor, with no accessories except for one roped tire dangling from a corner. The first time we saw him he had upchucked his veggies on the floor and was carefully picking through the bigger pieces. Though revolted, the crowd remained. Sure enough, after selecting his appetizer, he ate it again.

The second time we went, though I don't recall the occasion but it must have been special, Daddy was wearing a suit and tie. As usual the silverback had an audience. This time he had taken a huge dump in the middle of the cage and was playing with it. Someone shouted for him to taste it. Suddenly, without warning, seemingly planned, he grasped a huge handful and flung it through the bars at the horrified onlookers. Gorilla shit flew everywhere. People scattered. Being little, the smelly missiles caromed over my head. One piece though, landed squarely in the middle of

Daddy's tie. We laughed a long time about that. Of course, the next time we went, a sheet of plexiglass shielded viewers from further assaults.

On the weekends it was time to party. The usual watering hole was a place called Arkie's Corral. Since they couldn't get a baby sitter, I came along. Country music was the theme, and so long as it was daylight I could stay, once the sun went down I was escorted to the back seat of the car and slept.

Arkies was a big blue rectangular building with country legends painted all over it. The entrance was right at the corner of the street. Just inside the door, to the right, was the juke machine. The bar stretched from one end to the other with the stage just behind and eye level with the bartender. Along the opposite wall, tables and chairs were set. It was a friendly place where locals gathered for gossip and companionship.

Mom called it interpretive dancing. After a couple of 7 and 7's she'd urge me to dance. I would begin a gyrating fling that included some tap dancing and hip jolts perfectly timed to the rythm. I always recieved high praise and considered myself a dancer.

***

Fight or flight. The inherited mechanism by which creatures survive. A widely postulated concept that has borne truth in time, instincts seem a genetic inheritance. When packs outnumber one flight is the thought. One on one, fight. But for humans, mindful beasts, there is fight, flight, or submit. Throughout history peoples have submitted to others. The pain of loss gives over to acceptance, gods and beliefs syncretised. For individuals the pain of loss changes outlook, hopes, and dreams. For both cultures and individuals thoughts and philosphies change. Thesis, Antithesis, Synthesis. Bitter compromise. Bitter.

***

14

That school in Chicago was a foreboding, intimidating structure. A monstrous 4 storied cement castle with bars in the windows. It housed all the grades from K-12 and served the major portion of the southside. Mom walked me the first day, since it was only a couple of blocks away. But from then on I walked alone. I don't know why, she didn't have anything else to do. I went there from first to half of third grade.

I have disjointed memories of time spent there. I remember taking my lunch money and walking across the street for the bun and spicy meat; stick ball and pitching pennies; the cruel winters.

There are two most memorable events. The day my teacher came into the room crying and sending us all home. The President had been assassinated. For several days I felt the fear and pain of the adults. It was the only topic. One could sense it was the end of an age.

Another event occurred in the winter. It was cold and snow was still on the ground. They let us out into the schoolyard for our morning recess. Suddenly, in one corner there was a commotion. Two of the high school girls were fighting cat and tails. I think it was over a boy. One girl managed to get the better of the other, badly, and in the middle of the school yard, reached under her dress and pulled her panties off. She then stuck them on the end of a stick and paraded the grounds.

Things got better and we moved into a small house at the corner of a busy intersection. A nice place with two bedrooms, living room, and kitchen. It had a big yard out front bordered by a wooden log fence. Two logs intersected by posts every ten feet or so. I had some playmates that lived a few doors down. I did the Cub Scouts. I was happy there.

Daddy got me my first dog. We called him Mike. A blondish, brown cocker spaniel. He died about a week later. Then Daddy got another one just like him. We called him Mike 2. A lively pup, full of energy. One day I accidentally opened the door and Mike shot out straight into the yard, past the tree, underneath the fence and into the street where he was immediately crushed by a bus. I was inconsolable. My Mom rushed out, the bus driver got out and picked Mike up. He approached, extremely sad and offered to get me another. Mom thanked him, and assured him it wasn't his fault. He left apologizing.

And then there was Lady.

One day Daddy was out making deliveries when he saw some kids throwing rocks at a dog. He scared the kids away and approached her. She was starving and bleeding from the rocks and very frightened. Daddy picked her up and brought her home. We cared for her. She was a mixed breed, black and white, with a curled tail that stuck straight up. We thought she was a circus dog. She knew how to sit, lay down, and stay. She would jump up on the windowsill and beg. She would even speak. She became my best friend and I loved her dearly. She stayed in my life for two years.

The beginning of the end for the Dennis family came suddenly. One night I was sleeping in the car, with Lady, outside of Arkie's. Mom and Daddy got in the car in a furious argument. She was flirting again. I jumped up into the front seat between them. After a few blocks, they started again at a stop sign. Mom shouted an ultimatum and got out of the car. She beckoned me to follow. There was a split second where both looked at me. She was my mother. But I often wish I had stayed in the car.

He drove off leaving us at the corner. Lady watched us from the back window. We walked and found a diner where Mom called a cab. When we got home, Lady was there to greet us, fearful with head bowed. She was panicky and knew something was wrong. Mom went to her bedroom and I laid down on the couch. I was crying. Lady became agitated. Where was the man who saved her? She came to me and stuck her nose to my cheek. I told her to go away.

I was asleep on the couch when I heard a terrifying wailing. It was Lady, underneath my bed. She was crying her life out. I tried to reach her but couldn't. She died that night, underneath my bed, with a broken heart. True friend, I loved her dearly. Always there when I needed her. And I told her to go away.

Earl came back the next day. We were all heartsick. He took her and buried her somewhere. Things were patched up for the time being, but I know to this day that the night I left with Mom, when I made the choice, I broke his heart too. For four years, the only real father I ever had, the only one that ever did things with me, and I still miss him. A good man.

***

You'd think that after 20 years in the Navy I'd be more organized. Broke, maxed credit cards, behind on my bills. What's wrong with me? At least I'm keeping my grades up at the University. But how can I reconcile my desire for scholarship with such a dismal personal portfolio? What does erudition do for someone with a disposition for incontinent behavior? There doesn't seem to be any more new bars in the area and I've worn out my welcome at almost every one I've been to more than once. Stereotypical drunk. Arrogant and condescending... pretentious, and I'm no more cerebral than the next village idiot. Just because I play a half decent game of pool, and only then if not truly tested because when faced with a real player I fold and crumble. Heart, heart, where's the courage and heart for the real challenges. With the booze I suppose. And what am I doing in college anyway? Why don't I just get a steady job and be a normal Joe? What's it doing for me?

Summer school. The only reason I'm going is to keep my federal loans since I dropped Accounting last semestre. Accounting, should have known better, too much emotional baggage, not even in my curriculum. Thought I'd taste it since I was married to an accountant once. She was a beautiful girl but too stoic for me, separate agenda's, not to mention a ready made family. It would be easy to say it was the kids, but the truth is it was me, then as now unfocused, confused, and desperate.

Look at the class I'm taking this summer. English Composition. I've always wanted to write and express myself. Purge the angst or at least learn how but I'm as old as the instructor and he's not quite the messenger I dreamed of. Pidgeon toed, hairy ears, with a whiney voice that reminds me of Scarlett's maid in "Gone with the Wind". And the selection of readings are smeared with the touchy feely embrace of the politically correct. He hasn't liked the last two drafts I've submitted. Seems I lack imagination. Well... let's see how he likes this...

I first met my ex wife at a line dancing contest. Dancing to " Boot Scootin Boogie," I thought she was cute the way she stayed on her toes to keep her knuckles off the floor. Attractive, with one eyebrow, orbital ridges, and protruding jaw, I was mesmerized how she managed not to drop that drool off her chin. Beyond my infatuations, I could never warm up to those braided armpits...

Her bridal sweatsuit, red, was specially made with a line across her chest that came up to my nose. It read, "You must be taller than this ... to get on this ride." The Maids of Honor had matching coveralls, pink, and t-shirts that said, "Will drink beer for food." For their portrait, the Maids turned their backs to the camera and bent over, each looking over the other's shoulder. Six derriere's, the size of trashcan lids, with six small worn circles in the right pocket from snuff cans, six smiling faces turned toward the camera, and add them all together... one set of teeth.

The reception turned out as a huge affair. A wide screen tv was set up in one corner of the barn so everyone could watch the big match between Hulk Hogan and Roddy Piper. Aunt Suzie, in a wheelchair, was right in front rolling cigarettes from a tin of Prince Albert. She was still recovering from a snake bite at last Sunday's church service. Uncle Rufus approached us and handed me two tickets to next weeks truck pull and asked me what my plans were for the future. I passionately explained my goals for continued education, my personal need for growth and development. He casually mentioned how I was a good catch (the

*third?), and how lucky we were to be able to use the barn again.
I thought it strange how she still had the same in-laws. Somehow
all her marriages had the same aroma.*

*After he left, my bride whispered," I'm so proud of you,
schoolin'all, lookin back, I think 5th grade was the best three
years I evah had."*

***

Summer, 1964

The boy and his mother were alone again. With few
possessions they had moved into a small apartment complex in
Hyattsville, Maryland, a place called Queenstown. Mom told him
that they were alone again but that everything would be allright.

That summer he and some other boys formed a friendship.
They would cross the field behind the complex and play in the
woods along the creek, fishing for crawdads, playing rock wars.
Sometimes they would look for soda bottles and turn them in for
5 cents each.

He would always buy comic books. Superman and Batman
were favorites, but a new style was emerging, Marvel comics. The
Fantastic Four, Spiderman, and the X-Men became staples in his
growing collection.

Mom had found a babysitter in the neighborhood. She would
often go out on Friday and Saturday nights leaving a tall pimply
girl in bell bottoms and greasy shirts. This girl brought friends
over and played the Beatles and giggled all night while he would
try to watch TV. He wouldn't tell about the friends if she let him
stay up.

One night the girls were doing something different. One
would sit on the floor crosslegged, breathe deeply several times
with her arms across her chest, and another girl sitting behind her
would say "NOW" and the one in front would hold her breath
while the one behind wrapped her arms around and squeezed.

She fell unconscious. Arms dropped and she fell back against the squeezer. A loosened button and jacked up shirt gave him a good look at budding breasts. The other two giggled as she twitched. Her eyes fluttered and after a moment she said "wow" and slowly sat up again.

He asked what they were doing. It was a game they said, and would he like to play? Yeah. He sat on the floor crosslegged.

"Now cross your arms over your chest." She said, glancing at the other two.

"What's gonna happen?"

"It's cool, you're gonna feel a real rush. Now start breathing deeply."

He felt her lean against his back and bring her arms around. Anticipation.

"When I tell you, hold your breath as hard as you can."

The other two came close on each side.

"NOW." She said. Her breath deep in his ear.

He held his breath as hard as he could. A ringing tingling feeling absorbed his body. He saw the girls smiling as the world slipped away.

He seemed to be floating. As the blood returned to his brain his senses slowly returned. Strange sensations were registering. He awoke lying flat on his back. As he struggled to sit up he felt that his top button on his jeans was opened and his zipper was half down.

"Wow, what happened?" he said.

"You were dreaming." she said, the others nodding.

They played the game for the rest of the night.

***

The colony of spiders had grown. Not being a domestic god I had left them alone thinking that they would keep the ants and roaches in check. An ecosystem of predator and prey I felt comfortable with. They were small light brown spiders who had learned to scurry upon my approach. But a new generation had arrived, their domain heretofore unchallenged, and seemed undaunted when I returned after two weeks time. The Matriarch, as I deemed her, first apppeared over the counter, spindly web tucked deep into the corner a foot from the kitchen window. It wasn't in me to remove her and her strings for survival. I watched her progeny take refuge in obscure corners. They had become my partners in a common endeavor, life.

Let him live I thought. Tackling the crusted dishes a teeny spawn, unseen web spread across the sink, slid from the overflow hole anticipating a meal. I turned the water on to scare him off. Doesn't nature's rains cause retreat? Stubbornly he held on midway over the sink. Sprayed and unbalanced on an unsteady web, I lessened the flow to allow an escape. Hesitating between hunger and fear he returned to the hole and hid. I washed the dishes careful not to disturb his abode but I was determined that he would have to find another spot. Regardless of species, one does not always survive where they settle and must move on either from danger, lack of sustenance, or, for the more evolved, peace of mind because, for humans, success is not always measured by mere survival. For some reason I thought of the Navy.....

0600

" REVIELLE, REVIELLE, ALL HANDS HEAVE OUT AND TRICE UP, THE SMOKING LAMP IS LIT IN ALL AUTHORIZED SPACES, NOW REVIELLE."

" SWEEPERS, SWEEPERS, MAN YOUR BROOMS, SWEEPDOWN THE SHIP FORE AND AFT, SWEEPDOWN ALL COMPARTMENTS, LADDERBACKS AND PASSAGEWAYS......DISPOSE OF TRASH IN RECEPTACLES PROVIDED FOR ON THE PIER....NOW SWEEPERS."

" MESS GEAR, CLEAR THE MESSDECKS, EARLY BREAKFAST FOR COOKS, MESSCOOKS, AND THE ONCOMING WATCH."

I was startled, in the top rack, I suddenly realized where I was. I listened to the ship come alive through my curtains. I had reported for duty the night before, exhausted from the plane ride, dragging my seabag up the brow saluting the stern and then the OOD, Officer of the Deck, and, as taught, held up my ID in my left hand and while saluting said, " Reporting for Duty Sir!"

The Chief smiled with hidden knowledge and said," Permission granted." He scanned my orders and asked the Petty Officer of the Watch, POOW, to call PN1 Mulroy to the Quarterdeck. Several minutes later I saw a hatch open. In slow motion, in geologic fashion came one of my future bosses.

He was fat. Short and fat. Breathing hard he approached the Chief and turned towards me. First impression was of a pear with legs. Scuffed boots that hadn't seen polish in months, wrinkled bell bottoms that stretched tight over enormous thighs. His dungaree shirt, sweat stained and filthy, barely held back the layers of fat that hid his belt. I noticed beads of sweat pooling in his third chin. He held out a filthy hand and said with a leer," Welcome aboard." He took me to a compartment in the bow of the ship, pointed to a top rack and said," That's yours and this is your locker here. Since it's Friday night nobody's here. We won't be able to do anything with you until Monday. I'll be leaving in the morning, only duty sections are here on the weekends so if you need anything just ask one of the guys O.K.?" I nodded. He waddled around the corner and disappeared.

After mustering the duty sections I listened to the sounds of my new home die down. I slid my curtains, climbed down over the middle rack, showered, dressed, and set off to explore.

***

I loved to watch the cartoons on Saturday morning. Rocky and Bullwinkle outsmarting Boris and Natasha, Mighty Mouse, Aesop's Fables, and Dudley Dooright were favorites. I was always up early, or at least before Mom. This particular Saturday morning she seemed to be staying in her bedroom longer than usual. When she finally got up to make me breakfast, she casually mentioned that there was someone she wanted me to meet. As I walked from the living room to the kitchen I passed her bedroom. That is when I first saw him.

I could tell he was tall. Sitting on the edge of the bed in his shorts, boxers, he had big feet, long white legs and white chest except around his neck which seemed to be as sunburned as his face. He was a cab driver. Blue veins were visible along his ankles and he seemed to have large bumps on the shoulder and back. As I passed, he began lighting a cigar, an El Producto Blunt. Suddenly, and confusingly, he started to erupt in a paroxysm of coughing. I stood there dumbfounded. I had never heard someone cough like that. I thought he was laughing. I started giggling as I saw his face becoming apple red. It took him a full two minutes to recover his breath and when he did he turned to look at me. No other glare has left a more permanent impression. For the first time in my life, frozen there in that moment, the most basic instinctual emotion swept through my 10 year old body. Fear.

Mom wouldn't let him beat me like he did my older two step brothers. Still, beat me he did. But it wasn't the beatings that bothered me the most. It was the mind games. Making me run to the store for four or five times before I could go out to play. Standing with my nose in a corner for hours at a time. Accclimating to his violent rages, as if scripted, on a nightly basis. Mean bastard.

Seventeen years later, after many battles and controversies, I had learned to love him. Despite differences we had reached a truce. Since I had joined the Navy he didn't have to see me as much and fondness grows with separation. It was a quiet drive to National Airport, a little overcast as I recall. Mom stayed home. My orders were to Japan for three years and somehow I felt the need to show affection. When he pulled the cab over to the curb I leaned over and kissed him on the cheek, gave him a brief hug and said," See ya later Pop."

***

Youth should be youth, and those who bend those minds to their will, are robbing the cradles of future minds and beliefs. And those who influence the elderly are robbing their past and dignity. But each of us, from youth to old age, in the art of self protection, are more skilled in the thrust and parry to defend and promote one's self interests when mind and body reconciles the pecking order. Strong bodies and weak minds versus strong minds and weaker bodies contend for position. For much of our history both has had influence. In each generation there has been the unseen battle for the souls of the next.

***

1982, June

This brings back so many memories. Wally cried when I stood up and saluted during Taps. It was a shame that Peter wasn't there, the oldest son, still in prison. Uniform wrinkled from 16 hours of flight with only two hours to spare before the funeral, I was still dizzy from the suddenness of his passing. Mom seemed to be holding up pretty well. I would have to send her more money each month now but that's okay.

I can't help but reflect. It's been nine years now since it happened. I wonder how she's doing. I can always look in the phone book. Should I? Shouldn't I? Should I?...

"Hi, Sunshine, guess who."

"Bobby?"

I've missed her voice...smile. I've missed her so much. I'm sorry. "Yeah. I'm home on emergency leave from Japan. Herman died. Thought I'd give you a call."

"It's good to hear from you. How's your mom doing?" Sincere.

"She's okay.... I got your number in the phone book. I was wondering if I could see you?"

"Sure. I'm living in Georgetown now. Let me give you the directions."

***

1965

We moved into an apartment complex in Kentland. Peter and Wally, my two older half brothers helped us move in. It was on top of a hill, the area was very hilly, alongside one of the main arteries, Route 202 or Landover Road, that lead outside of Washington, D.C.. We were inside the beltway so you really couldn't tell if you were in Maryland or D.C.. I suppose we were suburban but it was all city to me. The complex surrounded half the hilltop like a medieval castle, divided into 12 unit structures of three floors. Each unit had one or two bedrooms, a kitchen, bathroom, balcony, and den. On the other half of the hill was THE WOODS.

Our unit was on a bottom floor. On a good day we could see the Washington Monument from our cement patio. We had a formica kitchen table, a green recliner and gold cloth couch, and a large black loveseat. Only Herman sat on the loveseat, which was in front of the t.v.. It also had the black belt underneath it, always handy for the occasional beatings. I had twin beds in my bedroom and my own closet. Life became routine. Routinely stressful.

Every school morning Herman would be up at 6:00 sharp. At six thirty he would bellow for me to get up. At 6:35, without fail, I guess I never learned, the sumbitch poured a cold glass of water in my face. I woke up furious every morning. By six forty he was out the door to pick up his regular fares and take them to work. Mom would get up and see that I had some breakfast, mostly cereal, and send me off to school by seven fifteen. Herman would return and pick up Mom and take her to her Accounts Recievable job at Dart Drug by eight. He would pick her back up and drop her off at home by four and then retrieve his regulars.

Between 5 & 5:30 he would come home. The moment he came in he would boom " Gladys", but it sounded more like "Glaadeeeese", and stroll back to the bedroom. He would return without his sports jacket and settle into his chair. Soon after Mom would come out of the kitchen with a large glass of vodka and grapefruit juice, 3/4 vodka, and put it on the coaster on the table in front of him. Like clockwork, by the time he finished his first glass the shit would fly.

"GLAADEEEEESE". Tapping his glass on the table.

"What? You son of a bitch." Sitting at the kitchen table doing her crosswords. She was already well ahead in the liquor department.

TAP TAP TAP TAP TAP TAP TAP

She had always hated domestic chores. Stemming from her youth, it must have always seemed that waiting on others was someone elses job. Herman knew what he was doing.

TAP TAP TAP TAP TAP TAP TAP

"Goddam bastard, can't ave one minute in peace."

She storms over and snags the glass, spends a minute in the kitchen and returns with a new refill.

"Oh, thank you honey." he'd say with sickly sweet sarcasm. Long face and red cheeks peeking over his paper.

"I hope you made some money today." Now it was her turn. She walked over to the table and waved a handfull of bills at him.

"Be quiet Gladys." His mood now changing.

"You know we have these bills to pay. You didn't go to the track again did you?" Eyes flashing, accusatory.

"Godammit, I SAID BE QUIET." Voice raising.

It was about this time he would begin the Herman Hand Shuffle. Blowing deep breaths through pursed lips, face turning red, rocking back and forth, and at the same time hands rubbing his thighs in a mechanical, kewpie doll fashion. Preliminaries to an explosion.
Sensing the telltale signs, she disappears into the kitchen. His dinner had better be ready at the moment the third drink was

finished. Dinner for as long as I remember was for him, steak, Ribeye, and taters with greens. I always got the bones, if there was one. If not, it was hot dogs and spinach, fried baloney, or pissketti outta the can. Sometimes, if there was a big steak with a lotta fat, the fat was sliced off and fried for me. "MMM, here, fried fat is good for you". To this day I gnaw the bones clean no matter where I'm at.

The nightly arguments and screaming went on forever. I can't remember any quiet nights. Even at such an early age children know what is right and wrong. The incessant nightly tirades between two grown adults was not normal. I knew it. I wondered how these two people could love each other when the only bond was hostility and screaming, screaming, screaming, at the top of their lungs. I was ashamed to look at the neighbors. They knew.

On Christmas of my 11th year, I recieved a boom box from my father who was now living in Nevada and working as a dealer in the Casino's. It could record. I wanted to make a point somehow. So when Herman opened the door I surreptitiously walked over to the windowsill where I had placed the box and pushed the record button. The ritualistic coughing spell, the glass tapping, the escalating dialog culminating into a fierce shouting match and his nightly threat to throw his food into the wall was, naturally, all caught on tape.(I had cleaned his tater's from the walls on more than one occasion)

I waited until the next day. After he settled himself into his chair and the nightly dialog began anew I hit play on the recorder. It took a few moments before recognition registered on his face. Listening to his own voice, and Mom's, the baiting and sarcasm, the screaming, brought an unusual aspect to his face. For a moment there was an understanding, a realization of life and his living of it. Even Mom came out from the kitchen to listen. She even started smiling. I began to giggle. Then the mood changed.

My mistake. I saw his face turn bright crimson. He began the Herman Hand Shuffle with an intensity I had never seen before. Then he bellowed,"WHAT THE FUCK IS THAT". In a black rage he rose from his chair and backhanded me into the wall, marched over to the box and started to slam it into the floor. He spent a full two minutes demolishing the box over my mothers cries to stop. Still simmering, the bulk of his anger spent, as I sat in the corner terrified and crying, he grabbed his jacket and silently left. I suppose none of us like to confront ouselves. To see ourselves from a distance. The pain of seeing who we really are.

I wish I stilll had that tape. Not that it symbolizes good times, but as a message from the past. A message I could learn from and maybe understand myself better.

***

Summer school again. Thought I'd take a writing class. I like this teacher, he comes up with good projects:

Humankind

Robert E. Kenney
1600 Pennsylvania Avenue
Washington, D.C.
United States of America
North America
Western Hemisphere
Planet Earth

Dear Friend,

On the eve of the second millenium this letter has been placed within a satellite that will orbit the planet for fifty thousand years. It's purpose is to communicate, as a voice from the past, to the future inhabitants of Earth, and present our present state of affairs with regard to science, history, and civilization as we know it. Hopefully this message will be recieved as an ancestral gift; a Rosetta Stone from the ancients, accentuating and confirming the continuous story of our species. Should the reader have no prior knowledge of us, let this serve as a testimonial of our existence, and extinction, whether by our own hands or from an unavoidable natural catastrophe.

Geological evidence suggests that this planet, third from the sun, first formed approximately 4.5 billion years ago. Fossilized organisms in the form of bacteria have been dated to 3.4 billion years ago. Since then the parade of life has evolved and flourished to every corner of the globe, creating, at least to date, one species that has dominated through adaptation and intelligence, the entire sphere. The scientific name, *Homo sapiens sapiens.*

Archeological records reveal that our earliest ancestors emerged from the savannah grasslands of East Africa some 5 million years ago. We distinguish ourselves from other animals through certain characteristics; Bipedalism, a two footed gait and erect posture which frees the hands for other purposes; Binocular vision, along with a decrease in facial features and tooth structure, that enables acute visual perception; And an enlarged cranial capacity, coupled with the free use of hands, allowing for innovations to overcoming environmental obstacles through the building of shelters, accumulation of resources, and the making of tools. It is that last feature which most separates us from any other species. We are the Toolmakers.

Inherent to our growth and development is our desire to define, communicate, and understand our world. This, as well as the physical and racial differences, has wrought the fundamental features of commonalities in societies, and the differences between them, Language and Culture. Separated by space and time, pockets of humanity evolved according to their own environments, established their own forms of communication, and built civilizations centered upon their own deities and cosmologies. For us, the line between history and prehistory occurs approximately 6000 years ago. Those who maintained written, physical, or painted records can be resurrected and theoried upon their world view, and those who did not remain recondite images within the passages of time.

Agricultural, sedentary societies grew to become Nation States. These Nation States provided the relative stability and security for individuals to devote energies toward the Arts, Music, Religion, Philosophy, Medicine, and Science. Explorations outside their domains initiated contact with other civilizations, encouraged trade between far flung peoples, exchanged beliefs, discoveries, and inventions. Though the mind of man has been nourished during times of peace, many discoveries, changes, and influences have been made under the duress of war. Persons and places identify crossroads on the map of history: Thermopylae, Alexander the Great, The Great Wall of China, Ghengis Khan, The Pyramids, Rome, Marco Polo, Columbus, Jesus of Nazareth, the Walls of Jericho, Aristotle, Stonehenge, the Parthenon, Buddha, Copernicus, Hiroshima, Michaelangelo, Jerusalem, Beethoven, Napoleon, Constantinople, Hitler, Joan of Arc.

From Galileo's telescope, proving that the Earth revolved around the sun, to Oppenheimer's nuclear bomb, unleashing atomic fission, the last 500 years has been an explosion of scientific growth. Generation upon generation, scholars added to the foundations of knowledge laid by their predecessors. Famous names and inventions signify paradigm shifts in our collective mind and lifestyle changes for future scholars and scientists to build on: the printing press, Darwin, the internal combustion engine, the microscope, Freud, the Hubble telescope, Marconi, Wilbur and Orville Wright, the telegraph, Thomas Edison, the Internet, Thomas Jefferson, Radar, Einstein, Television, Neil Armstrong.

The last major conflict, World War Two, just over fifty years ago, left the United States the predominate power. A Democracy, the United States was founded in support of personal freedom, freedom of religion, and the pursuits of happiness. This concept, Democracy, has proven the most fecund environment for not only the personal growth and development of individuals but for Humankind as well. Quantum leaps in the quality of life can now be measured in generations. But that quality does not extend beyond the industrial nations.

As of this month, it is calculated there are 6 billion souls on this planet. Yet, with only 6% of the worlds population, we consume 25% of the available resources and energy. The worldwide use of fossil fuels has eroded the ozone layer which protects us from the harmful effects of ultra violet light. The dumping of waste product into the waterways and the use of insecticides threatens the food supply and environment. Mass destruction of rainforests extinquishes vital ecosystems and species, some of which have been unrecorded. But possibly even more important is the death of coral reefs which may, due to their sensitivity to temperature, signal the onset of Global Warming, a potential catastrophe predicted by scientists over two decades ago.

As the year 2000 nears it may be necessary to find alternative energy sources as well as protections for the environment. We know that fossil fuels will be depleted by the middle of the next century. We don't know what the implications are for future generations if we continue to destroy vital aspects of the planetary ecosystem. As Nation States, Countries, and Governments found it necessary to protect themseves from each other, we should now prepare to protect ourselves from a new enemy, ourselves.

During my lifetime I have enjoyed the labors and accomplishments of a species some 5 million years old. I've sailed the oceans, flown in a plane, drive a car, read by lamplight, own a television, talk on a telephone, and have processed this letter on my computer. I hope and pray that we will continue to grow and prosper, but with a vision for the future. A vision that includes all of Humankind, hand in hand, reaching for the stars. Let us add to the arsenal of the Toolmaker, creating more devices which serve as the prosthetic of the human mind. As future generations move forward, let them draw from our contributions to the corporate knowledge as we have from the past. As Neil Armstrong, the first man to walk on the moon, said,"One small step for (a) man, one giant leap for mankind".

Your Friend from the past,

Robert E. Kenney

P.S. If you're a bug, forget I said anything about insecticides.

***

I loved school. Not just to escape the homestead, but always. Learning seemed to be central to me. Though extremely shy, my unwillingness to speak up never intruded with the absorption of what the teacher had to say. Still yet, my grades did not necessarily reflect a stellar student. History, English, not so much the difference between adverbs and pronouns of, and Biology or science in general were my favorites. It was in school where I came in contact with humanity, made friends, and learned social graces. It is in school where one learns what the world is all about and where we came from. But it is not just in a formal school where one learns about life. Schooling comes from many quarters.

The next spring we went to visit Aunt Nanny. She was getting very old and Mom was in her will. She lived in the rural farmland outside of Rocky Mount, North Carolina. I had never seen her before. She owned a lot of land.

Mom and I took the bus. I always liked bus rides. I would gaze at the countryside and marvel at civilization for hours. There was always a story behind every house, dilapidated barn, or highrise. There was always a person there whose life was somehow reflected by the farms, towns, and cities. I loved it all.

Her house was way in the boonies. A two story regal structure, for its age, that had been the palace of the Mannings, my mothers maiden name. It had a porch protruding from all sides with chairs and the ritual swinging seat for two. I marveled at it. But not because of its unique architecture nor any aesthetic splendor, but because of how the whole thing rested on wooden stilts which raised it some three feet off the ground. Lots of places to hide under there.

Aunt Nanny was the matriarch. Now old and withered she still commanded the attention of her many relatives. Staunchley religious she was the refuge to whom all would rely for not only moral but any other guidance.

"So you're Bobby?" She said approaching me with her aluminum walker.

" Yes maam."

"Let me have a look at you.... Hmmm... well now, what is it you want to be when you grow up?"

"Well... I'd like to be a scientist.... or maybe a preacher."

From that moment on I was on her A list.

Aunt Nanny and I hit it off. Mom even arranged for me to sleep with her in the most comfortable and soft goosedown bed I have ever slept in. At night, she would whisper knock knock jokes to me and we would giggle ourselves to sleep.

"Knock Knock?"

"Who's there?" I'd say for the unpteenth time.

"Humus"

"Humus who?"

And to the tune of that Humphrey Bogart movie song in 'Casablanca'.

"Heeuuw muss remember this..., a kiss is still a kiss..., a sigh is just a sigh."

It was the first time I had ever really been in the country. Distant cousins lived all around within a 2 mile radius. Most worked the lands planting tobacco and raising pigs. PEEUW. One day when I was bored I decided to explore underneath the house. I got down on my hands and knees and just about 5 feet in I noticed something land on my left forearm. It was a huge red wasp. I stared in horror, frozen, as I watched the monster dig its stinger into the center of my arm. I knocked it off and scrambled back the way I'd come screaming the whole way. Mom met me at the door and rushed me into the kitchen to run some water over an already angry welt forming. Aunt Nanny appeared and directed Mom to the first aid kit. But instead of putting some cream or ointment on the welt she simply pinched out a sizable portion of tobacco she'd been chewing and placed a bandage tightly over it. It worked. Despite the attack from a particularly nasty bug I was good as new the next day. And from then on I would have a quarter inch circular, tobacco stained mark in the center of my left forearm to remember her by.

We stayed for about three months, and, during that time, Mom enrolled me in the one room school house with the local kids. There was only about 18 kids ranging from 1st to 12th grades. The teacher gave many lessons to groups that composed more than one grade. I recieved high praise for my scholastics so that when the school year ended, even though I had started in the third grade, I would be graduating from the fourth. I think Mom had something to do with that. And when it was time to go I remember Mom saying that we'd come to visit again next year. We didn't know we'd never see Aunt Nanny again.

The sad day came and Mom and her two sisters got together and flew down to attend the funeral. When she returned there were animated discussions with Herman. Apparently, for Mom to realize any money, the land she inherited with her sisters would have to be sold. But the sisters didn't want to sell. They were well off and inclined to keep the land. I sensed bad blood the day Mom convinced them she needed the money. Things between them would never be the same. Still, Mom was thrilled to relay to me that Aunt Nanny had left me 10,000 dollars, a princely sum, not to be touched until I was eighteen, at least not directly.

***

Fancy said it was time I got outta the house. I had been invited over to Sugar's for dinner. As I followed her to her truck her wings waved broadly, shimmering a bright green. She seemed happy.

In the weeks since my release from the hospital I had taken long walks through the park and a few trips to the store. I began to understand the meaning of the colors in wings. The orange yellow of a schoolgirl reading a book beneath a tree, the angry red of a store manager scolding a clerk and her brownish red and pink of fear and embarassment. Blue for contentment, darker in strength and courage, gray for sadness, and green for happiness. There were variations in everyone, different hues, shades, and colors the combinations of would take time to interpret correctly.

" Sugar wants to start the team up again." Fancy looked at me, " Cherrie's comin back from Vegas, guess she misses home. " Two years should be long enough to know if you'll survive I thought,

" When's she due back? " Fancy said sometime before the fall league starts. Her wings had streaks of cold blue in them. Her eyes too. I had seen THAT look before.

Sugar represented the American Dream. Despite an abusive childhood, son of a mean plumber, the middle boy of two girls, he had suffered the stoic philosophy of his fathers' misogyny buffered by the love and protection of his mother and sisters. When he was old enough, leaving his little sister and mother to suffer the King's wrath, he moved out. Working for a local moving company he grew broad and strong. In two years he was foreman of his own crew and eventually foreman of the dock. At a wedding reception for one of his boys he had met Candy. The attraction was magnetic. They married and had twins.

Fancy pulled behind Sugar's truck. I'd often admired his place, small as it was, it still had Candy's gift for growing things. Perennials, annuals, roses and carefully tended bushes made her house the most attractive in a most modest neighborhood. As Fancy and I emerged from her ride two ten year old girls slid from the front door with a blonde cocker spaniel that yelped and scrambled in my direction. I knelt to his greeting.

" Hey Rums." I said, eyeing the twins approaching. Rums, or Rumplestilskin, had been my birthday present to the girls on their eighth birthday. Brown haired, like mother and father, and brown eyed like mother, they were destined to have their mother's classic beauty as well as disposition. Sugar, though proud, dreaded the future.

" Hey Booger Breath. " It was Ruby, the most aggressive of the two, singularly noticeable with the mole on the left side of her chin, grabbing my left earlobe with her right hand. "Yeah Cheeser." Said Opal, grabbing my other ear, " Where you been? " I released Rums and hugged them knuckling their ribs for giggles and said, " I've been to the moon and back, CHICKEN LIPS." Each gripped a hand and led me to the door while Fancy followed.

Sugar, filling the doorway, gave me a hug as we entered. Looking up at his hardened face and sandy hair I sensed a tenderness normally reserved for his ladies. His big hand, in the center of my back, gently pushed me into the living room. Before he could speak Candy was there cradling my face with her hands, tears in her eyes, dotting my face with kisses. " You guys better not pamper me, " I said, " What's for dinner? " Candy, straightening up to almost eye level and in her patented southern accent said," Geeoorgia Steeuw meester fancy pants..... and yewl like it or eelse."

I heard a toilet flush. The twins, glancing back at me with a strange look, quickly evaporated to the back yard with Rums. Candy retreated to the kitchen as Sugar bent to my ear and, with a growled whisper, said," You know who showed up this morning for an unannounced visit." Thoughts of a pleasant dinner suddenly dimmed.

Aunt Blanche wobbled around the corner and said," You need more toilet paper.", in her grating tone. Uncharacteristically, though reminiscent of past visits, Candy ingratiatingly told her Aunt, " I'll take care of it." The bitch moved towards Sugar's chair in front of the TV turning her head in our direction. Eyes settling on me she said, with unveiled sarcasm, " Oh, it's YOU." Fancy, cheeks red, grabbed my hand and led me to the back yard. Her wings were beaming a deep and scary crimson.

***

I have always loved old women. There's something special about them. It seems to me that old men maintain traditions but old women sustain our culture. They breathe life into civilization, bear the children, and nurture our inner minds. It is through old women that one might sense the finer aspects of the past and leave us with an optimistic vision for the future. But just as there is variation within every species, just as there are differences between brothers and sisters, so too do old women differ like the seasons, the weather, or day and night. Like Grandma Kenney.

Whenever Grandma Kenney came swooping in for a visit, the entertainment never ceased. Her graying hair couldn't diminish her bright mirthful eyes nor her aging body her mischievous grin and earthy humour.

She was Herman's mother. Unlike his dour, angry demeanor, Grandma had the ability to lighten up a room with her wisecracks and salty language. She had to, being married to Herman Sr.. Though Sr. had died several years earlier, tales were still being told about him being one of the meanest and nastiest men ever born. Figures.

Mom and Grandma could sit at the kitchen table and gossip for hours. Mom ritualistically rising every few minutes to step to the refrigerator, where she kept her vodka and grapefruit drink, and take a sip, and Grandma sipping on her beer.

"Cocknocker. When's that bastard gonna pay you the money?" Grandma referring to a gentleman that owed Herman.

"He say's he's strapped until he can dig from the bills." Mom said.

Then there was a series of grunts, depending upon the number, that would display just how much displeasure they were feeling.

"UMPH, umph umph!"

And Mom would repeat,"UMPH, umph umph."

"He can't even give you a little bit?"

"Nope."

UMPH, umph, UMPH, umph umph!"

"He's even got himself a new cab now." Mom says with intensity.

"UMPH, umph, UMPH, umph, UMPH, umph umph." Grandma grunts incredulously.

At night Grandma would sleep in the other twin bed in my bedroom. And until I would beg for mercy, she would tell me the nastiest, dirtiest jokes I have ever heard. Boy she knew them, having been around since WW1. There was one particular poem I made her repeat a dozen times:

> Hail to the Kaiser, that sunuvabitch
> May his peter be eaten by the 7 year itch
> May his balls be beaten by the American Hammer
> Till his asshole whistles the Star Spangled Banner

TuTu, Aunt Nanny, and Grandma Kenney were different women with different values and realities. Yet each, in their own way, symbolize the intangibles of what their generation left to mine. In that sense, consider them the Salt of the Earth. By the way, What is a COCKNOCKER?

" The Lord prefers common looking people. That is the reason he makes so many of them." - Abraham Lincoln , attributed.

***

Robert Earl Kenney

Jefferson's Agrarianism and The Myth of The Heartland

Central to American thought and ideology is Jefferson's Agrarianism and the intangible Heartland. Jefferson's answer to Crevecoeur's "What is this new American", was the subsistence farmer citizen. The farmer citizen would be the backbone of the republic symbolizing the freedom and individualism of this new American. The Agrarian republic would break the bonds with Europe and establish it's own separate identity. It was this vision that set the course for this nation, but it was a vision that would never reach fruition. Events would overtake this vision, events that could never have been foreseen, yet the vision still lives through the myth of the Heartland.

In 1803, Jefferson secured the Louisiana Purchase. In one bold strike he doubled the nation and by 1820 fully one fourth of the nation's peoples lived in the west. The expansion was paralleled by the Industrial Revolution. With the arrival of the steamboat and the railroad, the time between distant points was shortened. It became profitable for the farmer to expand his fields, and export his goods without fear for the perishable goods As farmers grew, it became apparent that business opportunities flourished within the realm of agriculture. Thus farming became commercial enterprises

As waves of new pioneers traveled west to realize their dream, the line between civilzation and frontier moved inexorably west. Much of our national vison is focused on a past of rugged individualists who braved the harsh conditions and tamed a wild and fecund country. In 1862 the Homesteaders Act reaffirmed Jefferson's vision. 160 acres per person were offered to settle unclaimed lands. But obstacles stood in their path. The Great Plains. Here rainfall was inconsistent at best. Despite professional theories such as " Rain will follow the Plow " , weather patterns such as the 20th isohyet were unyielding factors in establishing permanent settlements. From one third to one half of these citizen farmers were forced to sell or quit within 10 years. The individual farmer was replaced by the scientific expertise of a new movement, Agribusiness

By the end of the 19th century, Jefferson's vision of an Agrarian Republic had completely disappeared. Certainly small farmers were present but the dominant force was the entrepreneurial enterprises of commercial farming. Still, many of our values are sustained by the cinema. Movies such as "Shane" perpetuate that sense of the farmer who brings civilization to untamed frontiers. These intrepid souls did indeed exist but they were short lived and quickly replaced by the onslaught of the Industrial Revolution and the market forces it brought with it

I have often used the term "Salt of the Earth" to describe, in my mind, that vision of a segment of our society that has persevered and sustained the values, the true American values, that I consider the foundation of our nation. This term is often accompanied with another, "The Heartland", symbolizing that vague area where these cultural beliefs are stored and continued.

Mythmaking is the tool by which values are created, supported, and sustained. They also empower us and give a sense of belonging. 175 years after the Pilgrims landed there emerged the story of Pocahontas which was embraced as a true rendition of events heralding , and giving substance to, the rights of these new Americans to be here. So too is the myth of the Heartland. But Myths are not reality. Though Pocahontas was real, the events attributed are not. Though the cowboys were real, the exaggerated impact that they have on us is not. Painful as it is, the myth of the Heartland is only that, a myth

The Citizen Farmer may not have come to pass, but it was this vision that catapulted this nation into what it is today. Eager immigrants courageously forging west to establish their footholds were quickly overrun and replaced by entrepreneurs and big business enterprises. This scenario was repeated over and over again until there was no more frontier by 1890.

If anything, this class has managed to enlighten and take another look at these beliefs. It was not just religious freedom that initiated the quest for the America's, but land and the opportunity for wealth. It was one's personal wealth that ensured salvation. To be good and prosperous on the Earth provided the ticket to heaven. And it was this vision that seemingly overran the citizen farmer.

But it was the need to establish a national identity that forced these legends upon us. Stories that could relate common beliefs with disparate ethnicities and peoples. Fables which magnetized us into one purposeful value system. Romanticizing those elements of our past that most served to unite than diffuse.

Being of an older generation, the Disney generation, much of my earliest teachings have been in support of those myths which have served our nation so long. But I believe that Benjamin Franklin was not necessarily the kindly, gentle old eccentric statesman; Thomas Jefferson not a paragon of virtue; Our ancestors on the Mayflower not completely without capitalistic urges. Having been through the cabbage patch I realize that humanity is not without fault

I have always wanted a college education just to prove I can. There is benefit in placing the template of formal learning over the base of experience. If one aspect of this collegiate adventure is to think for oneself and question, the value of age allows one to think in retrospect and answer.

I will continue to use terms such as "Salt of the Earth" and "Heartland". Not so much because those peoples I refer them to are citizen farmers but because they represent to me what real America is. Not so much because a "Heartland" exists but because it suggests a source for all those things I admire in America. Besides, it makes me feel good.

***

One day we took Grandma to see Uncle Dewey, Herman Sr.'s little brother.. Uncle Dewey had been in prison for more than 40 years, and , in leniency for a life sentence, seems he had killed a man with a shovel, was being released. We went to pick him up.

It was a minimum security facility, in his seventies Uncle Dewey was no threat now, where the inmates lived in modest comfort. Uncle Dewey was even allowed to spend his time at a shack back in the woods where he kept a gazillion cats and a mess of chickens. He had names for all of them but declined to introduce them since half his tongue had been cut out many years earlier. The impression was he didn't know when to shut up. He didn't want to leave. I could tell by the way he fussed over his charges, worrying about how they would be taken care of. It was strange, my first visit to a penal institution, but not my last, and not the strangest.

It was a hot humid drive back. All the windows were open to alleviate the heat. Uncle Dewey sat between me and Grandma with Grandma right behind Herman the cab driver. We were about a half hour into the trip, in relative silence, when I saw Herman reaching into his pocket for an El Producto Blunt.

Him and his cigars. One's not supposed to inhale those things but he did. And due to years of those things it was a common event to hear him coughing his lungs out. Throughout the house there were the ubiquitous kleenex boxes with paper bags shoved into them with the tops folded down, mini trash bags whose main purpose in life were for the mouthfuls of phlegm Herman hacked up. But in the cab, there was the window.

He had a good burn working on that stogie and it was several drags before his body started reacting. Shoulders would start shaking first, and, depending on how deep this attack would be, you could tell by the length of time before breaths, and how quickly his face reddened, just how many chest oysters he'd be spitting out. I could tell this was gonna be a good one.

Herman had always been a careful driver. Even recieved awards for 25 years of a spotless record. But this attack was debilitating. Crippled for breath and reaching for the kleenex box on the dash he dropped the cigar into his lap. Dedicated to staying on the road and frantically reaching down to rescue his nards he half heartedly huffed a monstrous mouthful of lung butter out the window which momentarily hung there before being caught in the slipstream.

Uncle Dewey and I followed the flight path. The gob suddenly shifted gears and steered itself back into the rear window slapping Grandma right in the face with a 65 mph THWAP. Eyes widened in astonishment, face wrinkling with disgust while her hands began digging in her purse for a kerchief she said,"COCKNOCKER!". It was then that Uncle Dewey looked at me and our eyes met. We doubled over with laughter.

Uncle Dewey wouldn't let it go. He kept pointing out spots in her hair and on her dress so that by the time we got home Grandma was infuriated.

For his first meal out of prison we wanted to give him something special. But there was a catch. After years of caring for his chickens, he had seen one too many eggs laid. And for that reason he couldn't even smell eggs without gagging, and don't even think about fried chicken.

"What are we gonna have for dinner?" Mom said.

"How about some Chinese food." I offerred.

"Sure, let's get the usual....fried rice....lo mein... and maybe some Pork Egg Foo Young."

I turned to Grandma and said," Uncle Dewey doesn't like eggs though."

"Fuck Him." She said.

Mom called in the order, gave me the money, and I dutifully walked the two blocks to the restaurant. When I returned, all were sitting around the kitchen table reminiscing. When the plates were served, I took mine into the living room, Uncle Dewey said,"Whath thith?" And Grandma said,"It's a new dish made of something called Tofu, this here's Pork Tofu Young." I silently smiled as all four of them ate their meals. A lack of sympathy became a Kenney tradition when one of their own was emancipated.

Uncle Dewey left for Pennsylvania to live with relatives a few days later. I never saw him again.

***

The next two years, yet still with the nightly screaming and arguing, involved what my mother did with her money. Herman and some of the other drivers felt that they could strike out on their own and started a new cab company, Union Cab Co.. They rented a gas station, hired a mechanic, installed a radio station, and set out to compete with the larger, more established local company. And because Mom had invested a considerable amount, and had a large number of shares, she became the Treasurer and Herman the Vice President. Wise move.

During the summer I would work there pumping gas, changing tires, and, with guidance, perform maintenance on brakes and carburetors. I was earning a little money every week though Herman kept part of it towards when I became eligible for a drivers license. I enjoyed it. Though I never saw any of the so called saved money.

It was during this time that I also started going to Palmer Park Junior High. 7th Grade was radically different from elementary school. There was a core class where all would show up in the morning and be counted, and from there the class would, when the bell rang, proceed to another classroom with a different teacher. Everyone going to 7th grade was placed according to scholastic achievement. Classes were numbered 7-1, 7-2 all the way to 7-15.

It was a common belief that those placed lower than 7-10 were probably dumber than road apples. I was in 7-3.

Those were delicate years. Hormonal changes caused new interests in girls. It was not unusual for a teacher to ask a young man to step in front of the class and when he turned around, have a boner for all to see. It was also a time when the girls were establishing their persona's. My particular class had a few whom considered themselves quite prim and proper.

These were also years in which, it seems to me, young minds are building their own philosophies and cosmologies. In many ways the growth of the individual mirrors the growth of civilization itself.

***

Introduction

Western Civilization, as we know it, began not with the birth of Christ, but with the sages of ancient Greece. The likes of Thales, Socrates, Plato, and Aristotle initiated the quest for rationalizing and envisioning the workings of the natural world and the makings of the supernatural. It is their works and logic, primarily Aristotle's, that had a profound influence on western thought and beliefs well into the 17th century. It is the battle between science and religion, in this case Christianity, which has dictated the growth and development of civilization, our view of the heavens, contact with other peoples, and our view of ourselves. The past is filled with ism's, philosophical schools and doctrines, that have colored the historical landscape with their epistemologies and ontologies; Aristotelianism; Atomism; Empiricism; Existentialism; and Rationalism are only a few. But it is Scholasticism, viewed by many with contempt, that by its doctrine of merging reason with faith, allowed the scientific inquiry which led to its dismantling and the emergence of its successor, Humanism.

***

One night Mom and I had pork and beans for dinner. After the usual tirade things settled down and we all sat down and watched TV. A couple of hours went by, with Mom sitting with Herman on the Love seat, and being intoxicated and sleepy, she suddenly cut a loud FART startling herself awake. Herman began waving his hand in front of his nose making a grimace while Mom looked at me saying,"Who fired that shot?". We laughed. Everybody farted now and then.

The next morning I was sitting in English class. Desks were arranged so that two sat together at each. Since the beginning of the year I had been paired with this prissy little bitch right in the front row. We didn't like each other.

Sometimes things happen to me and I don't, possibly due to cultural upbringing, show the appropriate remorse. Several minutes into the class, this one being a silent study for reading, and the teacher having left, I felt the natural processes in my bowels. Unable to get permisssion to go to the bathroom, I sat there and gritted my teeth. Sure enough it happened.

The first fart was a small one but I felt the whole room focus on the back of my head. My big ears turned blood red. I saw Miss Prissy tense up. It was an accident, I didn't mean it, but in my fluster, since the dike had been breached, the second fart came out full force. I was quivering with anxiety as the aroma reached my nose when the third and final fart erupted. I didn't know what to do. Somewhere in my mind I heard the words, "Who fired that shot?". I started giggling. Miss Prissy, sitting on my left, suddenly reared back with all the force she could muster and administered the first slap. Mortified and glancing about the room, I could see the wide eyed expressions on each face, I continued to giggle like a dumbass. The second slap was just as hard and brought me back to reality. Hoping for some relief, mentally shrinking beneath the desk, Prissy slapped me a third time just for good measure when the teacher walked in.

I sat in the back of the class, by myself, for the rest of the year.

***

Monday

Revielle passed and I rose to a new day. Waiting for my turn in the head I nodded to those faces I'd met over the weekend. I donned a new set of dungarees, cleanly pressed the night before, and spent some last minutes shining my shoes at the table when I first saw him. Personnelman First Class Llewellen.

As he entered the compartment voices lowered. Murmured acknowledgements of " Hey Louie " marked his passage. I looked up and saw a recruitment poster. Spit shined shoes and creased dungaree pants, unheard of, sparkling belt buckle and creased shirt through the pockets like the Officers he strolled in my direction. Deceptively tall I looked up to a Clark Gable mustache, crew cut, and kind eyes. I stood up. Scanning my appearance he said, " I've been waiting for you."

" QUARTERS, QUARTERS, ALL HANDS TO QUARTERS FOR MUSTER, INSTRUCTION AND INSPECTION."

Standing in the back row I surveyed ships company, divided by divisions, on the flight deck. The Chief stood in front, flanked by Mulroy and Louie. Starched and pressed khackie's he was the dominent member of our enlisted ranks, and in many ways more important than the Division Officer. I saw Louie whispering in his ear. He peered in my direction and I heard, saw, and felt him stutter," I, I, I, I'll se se se se wha wha wha what I ke ke ke can do." Oh God.

We stood at ease waiting for Officers Call to end. Mulroy lamented last weeks failing inspection in the compartment by the XO for overfilled laundry bags. His was one of em. Suddenly, without fanfare, Officers streamed from the hatches. Louie barked, " Ah Ten Hut! ", turned and saluted a small bespectacled man and said," All present and accounted for Sir." Lieutenant Commander Dumchit returned the salute and motioned for the Chief, Mulroy, and Louie to approach. Glancing at my watch I noticed we had already been standing there for twenty minutes. Five minutes later, with Dumchit's departure, Mulroy turned to us and said, " Don't forget we want 100% participation for the Red Cross and Navy Relief this year......Dismissed."

Louie motioned for me to come over. He looked behind me and yelled," Spanky!" I glanced back and saw a weasly guy with beady eyes break from his group and approach. " I want you to take our new man here and get him checked in." " Okay," said Petty Officer Third Class Spanky, giving me a grin," But you better tell Mulroy, he's scared shitless of the Fleet Inspection of the Office this Friday. He'll scream if I'm not there." The three of us turned to Mulroy and The Chief in an animated discussion. I heard, saw, and felt the Chief say," Tha tha tha that's final." I looked at Louie, he smiled and said , " You guys go ahead, I got it covered."

***

Some things symbolize change. Even if that symbol is a hairy cough syrup bottle. I remember my first inner change. Choosing to do something, which in my neighborhood, and certainly among my peers, would be considered anathema. I tried out for the yearly school musical. I couldn't help it, I couldn't take my eyes off her.

I call her Dancer. She only lived two blocks away from the complex but it may as well have been on the other side of the planet. Long straight blonde brown hair, intelligent features highlighted by, what I thought, were tasteful glasses that framed crystal blue eyes. But her best feature were legs. Shapely legs always draped in skirts and knee high socks. I drooled after her and when I saw that she had tried for a part in this years showing of 'Oliver', and having never said a word to her, I followed in the hope that we might meet.

Rehearsals were after school. We all gathered in the cafeteria/auditorium for tryouts. Knees buckling from stage fright, I sang selected pieces for the director and virtually collapsed in relief when the ordeal was over. Dancer performed flawlessly. When the cast selections were made all the major parts were taken, one by Dancer, and I, I was the understudy to, you guessed it, Oliver. Rehearsals would be three times a week for four weeks, and one week of five performances the first week of March.

It was the last Friday before performances and anxieties were high for the big dress rehearsal. The Director spent extra time running the cast through their paces and, after last minute changes, gave us a pep talk and wished us a good weekend. It was dark by the time I reached the castle grounds.

I could hear the screaming before I opened the foyer door. Dreading descending the six steps to our door, I quickly glanced up to see any notice of the downstairs battle. I rushed to the door and entered:

"WHOREMONGER, IF I HEARTELL OF YOU SEEING THIS WOMAN ON THE SIDE I'LL SELL EVERYTHING AND TAKE BOBBY WITH ME, HEY BASTARD, ARE YOU LISTENING TO ME?" Standing right in front of him sitting there with her finger in his face.

Oh God, I don't believe this. " I hope you know the whole neighborhood is listening."

Using my entrance as his cue, he was always smooth like that, Herman calmly drew out another Blunt saying," Na woman, I dunt know what de fuk you're talking about."

This battle wasn't over by a long shot, both were ripped, and I could see the taters on the wall behind the t.v. and the steak and plate on the floor beneath.

Mom turned back towards the kitchen and I followed. She quickly placed some hot dogs and spinach on the table while I poured out some milk. She then turned back:

She said." YOU BETTER BELIEVE WHAT I SAID WHOREMONGER."

"NOW DUNT YOU START AGAIN BITCH" Face red, hands shuffling," YOU DUN RUINED MY FUKIN DINNER, AH DUNT WANNA HEAR NOTHER WORD .....AH'M GOIN TO BED." With that he stood up wobbling and turned right into the hallway disappearing like a 6'3" penguin.

Mom said,"We're gonna get away from him, just you wait and see."

But Mom had been saying that for as long as I could remember. Somehow I knew that would never happen. He had been her first love, and the only one really. Besides, she had become too old to find another and Mom was the type who had to have a man. I listened silently thinking LIAR and when I finished my dinner I went and cleaned up Herman's behind the t.v..

I watched the tube in silence while Mom did her crossword puzzles at the table. After awhile Mom said,"That sonovabitch better be asleep." and proceeded down the hallway to bed.

It didn't take long. Minutes later loud noises could be heard coming from the back bedroom. I heard Mom say,"NOT TONIGHT YOU BASTARD, YOU'LL BE LUCKY IF YOU EVER GET ANY AGAIN.". I heard a lamp crash to the floor. I padded towards the back bedroom. "IF I EVER thump HEAR OF YOU thump SEEING THAT WOMAN AGAIN thump YULE thump FUKIN thump REGRET IT thump thump thump thump." I said,"Hey, is everything allright back there?" and Mom said,"GO TO BED BOBBY.".

The next day was bright and sunny. I rose and dressed, ready to make mischief with my neighborhood friends. Mom was at the table doing puzzles. She said," Where you going?". I said,"Down to Dexter's." And she said,"C'mere I wanna show you something.".

She led me back to her bedroom and turned right into the bathroom. From a brief glance into the lovenest I could see it was a shambles. Opening the medicine cabinet she produced a large cough syrup bottle. Looking closely I could see it had hairs, brownish gray, attached to it. "That bastard learned a lesson last night." she said. We laughed.

From then on there was a change. Subtle, but I could tell. There was still the same drunken tirades, the glass tapping, the bellowing, but there was a change. We kept that fukin hair encrusted cough bottle for years.

***

An Image of Change, The Interregnum

For 15 centuries the Ptolemaic concept of a geocentric universe was embraced by both the scientific, philosophic, and theologic communities. Imagine how the foundations of society shook when learned scholars dared to proclaim that the Earth was not the center of the universe, but rotated in orbit around the sun. The Ptolemaic/Aristotelian tradition challenged by new technology and methodology. The very cornerstone of religion robbed of its "Perfect" universe. Giant figures take part in shifting this monumental paradigm, Copernicus, Kepler, and Tycho. But little is known of the last great defender of the geocentric faith, Christoph Clavius, while his counterpart and contemporary, Galileo Galilei, is the universally known protagonist of the truth. It is during the mid 16th and early 17th centuries that the world shook and corrected its place in the mind of man. It must have taken tremendous courage for intrepid scientists to challenge the entrenched philosophies, but we know that in the end it was truth that triumphed, despite the machinations and persecutions of the adherents of the old order. This was a chaotic time in our history, it was an ending of one philosophical reign, and the coronation of another. An Interregnum.

In order to better understand this Interregnum, it is best to review the sequence of events which culminated in Galileo's retraction and incarceration at the age of 70.

Copernicus published in 1543, the year he died and 13 years after he completed it, <u>On the Revolution of the Heavenly Spheres</u> . In it he states that the sun is the center of the universe, that the previous 10 spheres of the geocentric cosmology was now only nine, and that the earth rotated around the sun and the moon around the earth. This was controversial at the very least, and knowing this, Copernicus dedicated his work to the Pope and, through another, proposed that this was only a theory. Still, it was denounced by both the Protestant and Catholic religions, and found little support for the next 60 years, primarily because of the complexity and required proficiency in mathematics it took to be understood.

To further confuse and confound, Tycho Brahe, without benefit of a telescope, yet with accurate tables of the sun and planets, proposed a compromise to both the <u>Heliostatic</u> and Geocentric systems. The Tychonic universe held that the earth was in the center with the sun in rotation and the planets rotating around the sun. This was rejected by his most famous student, Johannes Kepler, who believed that Copernicus was right but wrong to continue the mystical quality of the spheres. Then, of course, comes Galileo, as one of the first armed with a telescope, and proves that Copernicus and Kepler are right in their assumptions, initiating to his own detriment the wrath of the Catholic Church. But the damage was done, no recantation or blind belief could dispel the Heliocentric theory. It was a desparate time for the Church, profound discoveries disputing the Physics of Aristotle, the discovery of the New World, and the Earth's obeisance to the Sun served notice to the faithful that a new order had begun.

***

1967

A new school year. I was a bit disappointed at being placed in 8-2 due to year end testings, I might actually have to do homework. There were the same old subjects of History, English, Social Studies, gym and Art, but this year I had two new subjects, Algebra and French. There were some new faces some old. I was filled with a sense of optimistic anticipation.

Algebra. Dull and mind absorbing, the incomprehensibility magnified by a teacher whose monotone delivery ensured more daydreaming than concentrated effort. With a modicum of personality or at least SOME excitement in their own subject I might be able to pay attention enough to maintain a fair average, but this teacher was so bland I couldn't keep my eyes open. I knew early on that I was in trouble with this one.

French was intimidating too, at least at first. Mrs. Nair was a short bubbly middle aged woman whose accent gave away her European roots. Daily, in accordance with yesterday's assignments, we would repeat, after her, conjugated verbs and read assigned paragraphs. A stickler for pronunciation, she'd single out the worst offenders and make them repeat the word to her satisfaction. "Meeshell", she would say,"Repetay, SHOCK- 0- LAH, see vu play.".

At the beginning of a long weekend, after a period of recitals and instructions, Mrs. Nair, anticipating spare time for homework, said," Ohkay, pour zis veekend...". With the pause I raised my hand. "Whee Rowbear," she said," kess ke say?". And I said,"Repetay, see vu play... FOR THIS WEEKEND...". By the time the last word left my mouth a broad grin spread on her face as she made her way around the desk in my direction. The class erupted as she chased my happy ass around the classroom.

***

Language. That most special gift or tool possessed by humankind that forms the matrix of culture and the foundation of civilization, is most surely an area of study deserving of special interest within the field of anthropology. Of the earliest scholars that founded this field, Franz Boas and Edward Sapir, it is beneficial to note the times in which they lived, their careers, and the methodologies by which inferences and conclusions were made

Franz Boas (1858-1942), founder of the first anthropology department in America, is the originator of "Cultural Relativism", where all cultures are equal and comparable. He also stipulates that the presence of variability within phenotypes precludes any thought of inferior or superior races. As a German Jew reaching maturity during the age of Darwin and Huxley, subjected to the social and racial disparities of pre WW2 Germany, such conclusions might be made with personal profundity

Born in Germany and raised within an Orthodox Judaistic household, Edward Sapir (1884-1939) shared more than a scholarly bond with his mentor, Boas. Through his studies he established the Uto-Aztecan family of languages and emphasized the importance of the individual in culture. He also stressed psychological problems within culture. Sapir, "... argued that there is no causal link between a language and a culture. He regarded a culture as what a social group does and thinks... a language as a way of thinking.(Handout)

In "Introduction to the Handbook of American Indian Languages", Boas notes the difficulties of classifications with regard to physical type, language, and culture. He proclaims that all classifications of mankind are artificial in character. In it, he also cites the practical need of language for ethnographic studies,"command of the language is an indispensable means of obtaining accurate and thorough knowledge.(p.18)" The relationship of language and thought is discussed. I am left with the belief that not only a knowledge of the language is needed but at least some background in psychology to effect an insight to the recondite aspects of any culture

Sapir says that," All cultural behavior is patterned.(Blount p.31)" He defines individual and social behavior. Unconscious patterning in language appears to be a driving force of culture and behavior. "In spite of the fact that language acts as a socializing and uniforming force, it is at the same time the most potent single known factor for the growth of individuality.(p.51) I tend to agree.

But language must also be flexible and malleable. Establishing the placement of nouns and verbs, tones, morphemes, syntax, and semantics does not mean that a language may not fall into desuetude. It must have the ability of growth and development consistent with the ability of it's community. The concept of an international language may not be far off (Sapir p.63), though I don't want to discuss the problems of nationalism. As the world seems smaller through communication (i.e. language), humankind may naturally assimilate one language. Studying cultures in an assiduous manner must require that the scholar have the ability to communicate with the individual in their language. Only then can social and individual patterns of behavior be observed and interpreted accurately. An emic, or insiders, approach through language seems the best way to study the psychology of any biological, cultural, or linguistic unit

***

Saturday, and the boys were coming over for a poker game. It was winter and the horses weren't running. The cabbies needed some recreation. Herman came and picked us up to go to the liquor store. Sherriff's Liquors. A Mom and Pop operation where we got discounts since we bought from there at least once a week, by the case. We all got out and went inside.

The Adult candy store. Rows of intoxicants grouped by species; Gins; Vodka's, Whiskey's; and Brandies with Beers in the back. I always liked to walk down the aisles looking at the varied colored bottles and exotic names. There seemed to be more there than one person could ever try. Mixes and recipes with cool sounding names. This was something I could look forward to. I picked up a case of Gilbey's, as usual, and Mom carried the preferences of the other poker players. I loaded everything into the back seat along with a bag of ice while Herman joked with Mr. Sherriff and Mom gossiped with the Mrs..

We got home and prepared for company. Mom laid out a tablecloth over the kitchen table while Herman produced a couple of new decks of cards and the red, white, and blue poker chips. An empty cigar box was placed on the table to keep the money for purchased chips. After all was set we waited.

The gamblers arrived in short order. First was Teddy, an old family friend. I always called him Theodore to annoy him, in his mid thirties and a father of five, as big as Herman but more muscular and heavier. He was missing his two front teeth from a bar fight. Then Larry, dark haired and good looking with a way with the girls, always smartly dressed wearing colorful suede loafers. Packer appeared, as usual, with an air of self importance, thin, pale faced and balding, he was President of the company. And Jiggs, the classiest of them all, all of 70 years old, dapper with his fedora and cleanly pressed suit and everpresent bow tie. He was the only one who ever tipped me when I pumped his gas.

Once the game began it didn't take long for the conversation to turn to business. With the exception of Larry, the others were the most experienced drivers in the company and owned their own cabs. Company cabs were purchased from rental companies, painted, licensed, and rented out. The four were also the core educators in the art of dispatching. Knowledge of the streets and the quickest way to get from point a to point b is the bread and butter of the trade. Wasted gas is lost money.

"I had a good one yesterday." Said Ted," Fifteen calls on the desk and this guy calls and wants a ride to National Airport from 1106 Corinth Ave. Guess where that is?" "That's in Glenarden," Says Herman," Corinth, right off of Pine.". "WRONG." Barks Ted. "Sure." Says Packer," Corinth, connects Pine to Pepperdine, four blocks worth." "Wrong and Wrong." Says Ted, "What do you think Jiggs?". And with his kind and gentle voice he said," 1106 Corinth, that's a dirt alley off of Landover Road about a half mile from the beltway, I know the guy. He's an architect, bought the land before they built those apartments around him, his boy went to school with my girls, named his dirt road after his wife, must have been a big job to drag him outta there." Ted said," Shit Jiggs, where the fuck were you yesterday, I had Jackson look for him for an hour?" Said Jiggs," I had a date with twins.". Larry spoke up leeringly and said," Give me their number, I've never had twins."

Larrry didn't know those twins were his daughters and it had been their birthday.

Dispatching. Every enterprise has a nerve center, but in few is it more focused on one person, the Dispatcher. We all took our turns answering the phones, you'd write the customers address on the top of a slip of paper and the destination on the bottom. Then the Dispatcher would, depending on location, and his own mental mapping, place it on the table in front of him with the others. Once the job had been bid upon and accepted, he would write the cab number in the middle and place it in one of the slots in front of him with that number. This system enabled him to know how many jobs each cabbie had had and for the newbies he could follow them to each destination and lead him to another. A feel for the city and it's inhabitants was paramount to run a successful shift. It was always good to get in good with the Dispatcher since he could either "feed" or "stiff" you, especially the good fares. And, as in all enterprises, there are good apples and bad. Good customers and bad too.

The next morning I asked Mom who won. Jiggs had taken them all to the cleaners.

***

Interview with a Car Salesman

Buying a car is a major purchase. Most of us know what it feels like. Hoping for a good deal yet feeling helpless, vulnerable, and at the mercy of the salesman. Reading ads in the paper and, once there, finding the terms have changed or the car gone and being steered toward another. Asking simple questions like,"How much?", and never getting a straight answer.

I work part time with a gentleman who used to make a living selling cars. His friendly and kindly deameanor contrasts starkly with what one might envision for a car salesman. I asked if he would participate in this project and he agreed. During moments of idleness he provided the following:

Q. No remorse?

A. Well, I felt bad. Especially for those who didn't have the balls to say no. Some of the guys would say," hey they ain't paying your rent"..... You have to be pretty hard nosed when you go shopping or they'll stick it to you. It's the guy who's the skinflint that get's the deal. Buys the same car as the other person and gets a better deal because he's tighter with his wallet.

Q. How much profit do they make?

A. For most dealerships used cars are the most profitable. Actually, the profit comes from the amount paid on the trade-in.

Q. What are the best buys?

A. The Rental Fleets. Originally sold to be used as rentals, used for a year, and then sold back to the dealership. You know they've been kept in good condition. Serviced after every time it goes out...washed.

Q. How would one go about getting a good deal?

A. Do your homework on the car. Find out how much YOUR car is worth and then go to the lot after hours. Pick out something you like. When you go back the next day, describe what you want and see if they give you the runaround.

Q. How much commission does a salesman make?

A. About 25 to 30 % commission of the profit. Sometimes they even get paid on the financing too. There's pressure on not to keep any cars on the lot more than 60 days. Some are paid a bonus to get rid of it.

Q. What is this system they have where the guy you're talking to has to go see someone else to answer your questions?

A. It's called <u>Liner-T.O.</u> . The first guy, the <u>Liner</u>, approaches you and determines if you're interested in a car. Ride with you on a test drive. He'll ask something like,"If the price is right would you like to go home in this?". Then he'll do the turnover (T.O.) to a manager or team leader. He'll say something like,"this is my brother", or whatever lie works. Sometimes there's even another level.

Q. That kinda pisses me off. Especially when they won't tell you how much the car is.

A. Pisses most people off, but it works.... and he'll never tell you how much the car is. Look at those advertisements you recieve in the mail every month saying you're eligible for 2 thousand off. Ya think you're getting that....HELL NO. Those cars are already marked up.

Q. Do you think that's why they don't enjoy a good reputation?

A. In the past a lot almost HAD to be dishonest to make money. I only worked for those stores that were clean and honest. I couldn't be one of those suede shoe slicks...tell em what they wanna hear. I always tried to give'em the best price I could.

Q. I guess it comes down to the managements mentality, doesn't it? A lotta pressure?

A. Yeah, some of those whorehouse lots have no ethics. You're forced to be a liar. You might have a manager watching and if you don't T.O.'em it's termination on the spot. They want you to keep goin after em, none of this 'I'll come back next Tuesday' stuff.

Car Salesmen aren't viewed with the greatest prestige in our society. But I think the majority are hard working, honest, and sincere. As in any occupation there are good apples and bad. Just as there are good dealerships and bad. One must be prepared.

The only answer to a system that attempts to hold one hostage is to be armed with the information they don't want you to know. Look up the Blue Book price of your trade-in. Know the price of the car you want before you step on the lot. Be firm and resolute. Remember there are other lots in town. Or, have a relative in the business. Unless I'm mistaken, we only live once, and it would be nice to get it right the first time and not be taken for a ride we can't take back..

***

Our English teacher had us all line up against the walls. We were going to have a Spelling Bee. The winner would be in the school Bee Friday afternoon in the auditorium in front of the whole assembly. One by one students mangled their words and sat down until, inevitably, I was the last one standing.

Friday came and there I was sitting in front of the entire school with about 30 other students. One by one students would rise and stand at the mike and spell a word for the Principle, who was the moderator. The first and second place finisher would compete in the regionals. After about six rounds I was surprised to see myself still in the game with two others. My name was called. I rose and walked to the mike.

"Okay sir," said the Principle," Once again you're allowed three attempts, spell Book-keeping."

Hell, I thought, this one's easy," B-O-O-K-K-E-E-P-I-N-G."

"That's incorrect, you get two more tries." He said.

What? You gotta be kidding. Okay," B-O-O-K.......E-E-P-I-N-G."

" Incorrect, once more." Giving me a quick glance.

I was confused, something was wrong here. I said," B-O-O-K.....K-E-E-P-I-N-G."

"I'm sorry," he said, " The correct spelling is B-O-O-K... HYPHEN...K-E-E-P-I-N-G."

I couldn't believe it, I turned and sat down wondering where the hell that hyphen came from.

As soon as I walked through the door I marched over to the Queen of Crosswords and said, "Hey Mom, how do you spell...". She was on the phone," ...Well, I'm just calling around to see if we can locate him, he's been missing for two days now, he didn't even check out with dispatching and that's not like him............Okay, call me if you hear anything." She had a worried look on her face. I said," Who's missing?". Mom said,

"Jiggs, he was working the late shift night before last, seems he disappeared."

The phone rang, once. Herman must be dispatching. It was a standing rule to always wait for the second ring, one ring meant to call the company. Besides tying up lines with personal calls, the phone company charged extra for outgoing calls for a business that should be recieving only. Mom dialed the number. It was Herman, and, after a moment of silence, Mom started crying. Jiggs had been found. His cab had been located in an abandoned lot. He had been shot in the back of the head.

To this day I wait for the phone to ring twice.

***

Even mice, one of the less vicious of God's creatures, stands up. Like the poster of the mouse shooting the finger as the eagle approached, I've seen a mouse stand up. Reality is much more graphic.

I was helping a friend consolidate her yard. I had mentioned a love for dogs and she had gotten one. The frisky pup kept getting in our way. As we pulled a sodden plank of wood from the earth a mouse, home exposed, streaked towards the nearest shrub. The pup, a female juvenile, gave chase. She caught and grasped the rodent, shook it fiercely, and let it go. The mouse ran again. In play she paused and then pounced, once again waving her prey in the air. Released, the critter recognized its plight. Exhausted, I saw it sit back on its little haunches, stare the doberman in the eye, and squeak in ultimate defiance. Then she killed it. I never warmed towards that dog afterwards.

***

Anger and depression. A volatile combination, and fueled by alchohol, the perfect self punishing vehicle. Anger, for most, is a short lived event quickly cooled, self forgiven and forgotten. For me it is a daily expression, concealed, and yet expressed through innuendo and body language. But depression is an insidious malaise, striking mostly in solitude, evoking tears in even the most quiet moments. But what moments are quiet for an active mind? What mind does not live retrospectively in the subconscious? What past can be discarded to enable a rose colored view, an acceptance of humanity without dwelling on the flaws? How do I survive without hope, initiative, goals, and not the least, self respect?

There were three of them. They caught me leaving my downtown room and walking to the mart, mentally parsing my dollars to last another two days until my pension came in, by surprise due to the intensity of survival. There they were, in broad daylight, sitting on the church steps under the shade of the tree planted by the curb, across the street from the park.

The Park. One acre of wide open grass with a few trees thrown in. I avoided it , despite the wide open spaces, due to the rows of benches populated by the poor and dissolute who had no problem asking complete strangers for cigarettes and money. It was a gauntlet I had no patience for.

As I entered the shade equidistant from the tree to the steps the middle man spoke, " Hey, got some spare change?', holding up a crumpled dollar bill in his right hand. I glanced over, all three were my age but unshaven and unkempt. The one on the right had a black eye. I sensed danger, I know what it feels like. "Sorry," I said," I'm counting pennies too.". He said," We're just trying to buy that tree there.", cackling at his own wit. I continued on.

It occured to me that I was but one step away from sitting where he was. But I was a lifetime from being like him. I felt contempt, no pity, there was nothing pitiable about them. In darkness it is just such arrogant, and violent beings, who have no pity for others.

In my adult life I have always been wary of three strangers in the darkness.

I fear I have become a misanthropist.

***

If two men, born on the same day, live comparable lives and reach middle age, which, do you think sees the world more clearly? The one with family and friends or the one with the marred heart? Which sees the chance of catastrophy and which stability? Which judges more acutely the hearts of strangers? And which is more willing to help others in need? Which, do you think, would be more willing to sacrifice before the other? And which, of course, would be more liable to leave his mark upon this planet?

***

1968

It was that time of year again. The school musical. This years would be a production of Finian's Rainbow. And once again I followed Dancer to the tryouts.

This musical was about Finian and his stealing of a Leprechaun's pot of gold. So long as Finian kept the gold the Leprechaun would gradually become human. The three main characters were Finian, Og the Leprechaun, and a young maiden who couldn't talk but communicated by dancing. For four weeks I rehearsed as Og the leprechaun, with Dancer as my paramour.

One day, after rehearsal, I started walking home under a darkening sky. I had to cross the football field behind the school, pass through some woods, and wade across a wide pasture to get to the bridge and then home.

There were three of them. One was a red headed brat whom I'd seen at school. He confronted me as I approached the bridge. " Excuse me," I said, and started to walk around him. He stepped back in front of me and said," I don't like you.". I was shaken, I didn't even know this guy. I glanced at the other two and knew I was in for a fight. Then he pushed me.

I had only ever had one real fight, and that had been in third grade. I hadn't won. But this was now and I wasn't unarmed. The previous summer I had boxed for the local boys club. Several weeks of training for the first round tournament, from which, only winners continued the season. I hadn't continued the season. I had stepped into the ring with this blond haired kid and we duked it out for three rounds. It was several minutes before the judges made a decision. All agreed that the match was a close call, but they gave it to my opponent, last year's Golden Gloves.

He pushed me again. I stepped back and put my fists up and said," Okay fucker, you asked for it." I started dancing on my toes. I had surprised him, but only momentarily. He stepped forward launching a haymaker. I dodged it and, moving forward, clipped him on the cheek with a right cross. He came back at me and I bloodied his lip with a left jab. Then, furious, he ran at me and we grappled. We went to the ground. Somehow I managed to get on top. I broke away and quickly stood up. But because of the scuffle, when I stood up my back was to his friends. Without warning, one of the other bullies had come up behind me. I suddenly felt the impact of a fist on my right temple. Tears started forming in my eyes. The one who hit me said," Get outta here.".

I cried all the way home.

***

I've tried to outrun the past but I am nothing without it. It stays with me like a letter, seal broken, paragraphs read and reread unbidden. The good the bad and the ugly becomes a part of the measurement of us all. For me, a daily occurence. My strengths and weaknesses in the present are the results of my past. Personal failures and accomplishments measured by the scales of the mind. But it was one certain night that events loaded the scale to the negative. I've seen it in the eyes of others. Once self perception and worth is lessened, no peak ever equals a valley. I am forever the bended tree recovering from the storm.

***

The Iliad, a Patriarchal Document

The influences of ancient Greek culture is ubiquitous in western civilizations. As some ancient societies have deliquiesced into the compost of humanity, others, their cultures and values, are preserved. About 800 B.C., Homer, inventing the "Age of Heroes", transcribed 300 years worth of oral traditions and myths of an earlier peoples, the Myceneans, and produced the "Iliad"(WH, 33). Through this work, many of the values and beliefs, such as the role of the Father and the "Heroic Code", were embraced, symbolizing a glorious past while ushering in a new era

The "Iliad" tells the story of the fall of Troy. A ten year quest to avenge the abduction of Helen, wife of Menelaus and sister in law of Agamemnon, by Paris. The tragic hero is Achilleus, who depicts the epitome of the "Heroic Code" and it's values.

Throughout this epic the major players are identified as the sons of their fathers. Called patronymics, this concept is present in the first sentence, "Sing, goddess, the anger of Peleus' son Achilleus and it's devastation, which put pains thousandfold upon the Achaians,"(1, 1-3). As Zeus, the supreme father, commands the gods and directs the battle to his will, so too, the fathers command the sons to battle and direct their actions according to the code. As Peleus to Achilleus, Hektor to his infant son, or Hippolochos to Glaukos, the Paternal Injunction to "Be the Best" in battle, is a recurring theme. When Glaukos meets Diomedes on the field of battle he says:

But Hippolochos begot me, and I claim that he is my father he sent me to Troy, and urged upon me repeated injunctions to be always among the bravest, and hold my head above others not shaming the generation of my fathers,...(6, 206-209)

The immutable doctrine of the "Heroic Code" has many features. Strength or "Bie" over reason or cunning. The glory of combat, "Kleos", instead of the security of home. Contempt for technology, tradesmen, archery, and words instead of deeds.

But most important, Honor over material things, and , if sullied avenge it. For to die an honorable death against a worthy opponent, an Agon, is intrinsic to the code and deserves the fame and commemoration of a hero's death.......

***

Herman had learned a new word.

TAP TAP TAP TAP TAP TAP

"UMPH, umph, umph, ...I never get a moments peace." She said.

TAP TAP TAP TAP TAP TAP

" Cocknocker, ...I hear tell you went to the track yesterday."

" Listen bitch, I told you I was working. Don't <u>CONTRADICT</u> MEEEE." Hands started shuffling.

"That's what I heard goddamit, don't lie to me." She said

" I done told you, don't CONTRADICT MEEEE." Face red, breathing hard, shuffling.

I said," Can't you two get along? Don't you know this ain't natural?"

" BOYEEE, don't you CONTRADICT me TOOO!" He reached under the loveseat for the black belt.

It had been some time since he had beaten me. It's presence under his ass had become more of an anachronism. Reaching for it was a false threat. But as he pulled it out a half used pack of L&M's came out too. OOPS!

Mom had always kept her carton on the windowsill by the kitchen table. After my guardians left for bed, in their drunken stupors, I felt free to watch TV into the wee hours and to experiment. When I was little I could remember Mom buying me candy cigarettes and colorful bubble gum cigars. I began to experiment with hers. It was arrogance that caused me to keep the pack by the black belt.

" Well, what have we here? " says Herman, holding the pack up for Mom to see.

" I thought I'd been missing a pack or two. What is this Bobby? " Walking over and glaring at me.

" Just trying em." I said, caught in the act, " But I haven't been inhaling."

" Well BOYEE, have a seat here." Herman patting right beside him. I hesitated, but sat down.

Herman placed the belt between us, reached to the coffee table and slid an El Producto Blunt from its pack. He peeled the wrapping and ring off and said, "Here.". I took it. He said," Now lick it real good and bite the tip off.". I was embarassed. Mom, towering in front of us said," LICK IT.". I licked it, face crinkling from the taste. " Now bite the tip off." said Herman. I bit the tip off, spitting it into the kleenex/mini trashbag by the seat.

Producing his gold lighter he said, " Now light er up.". Holding the lighter for me I took some tentative puffs." Harder.", he said. I drew harder, getting a good start on the cigar. "Now draw and inhale.". When I sucked the smoke in, my lungs immediately rejected. I began coughing, spit drooling from my lips. "Do it again", he said. I did. Still coughing, I felt a dizziness overcome me. He made me do it again, and again, until a third of the cigar was ash before I bolted and ran to the bathroom. Green and dizzy, once finished, Mom said." Go to bed.". In my delirium I thought I heard laughter coming from the living room. I tossed and turned all night.

***

I was despondent. It was a week after the performances. Five showings of Finian's Rainbow, dressed in green tights, green beret, and lipstick, singing my bisquits off with Dancer as my onstage love. Still, I had never spoken to her, on, with her mute part, or off the stage. After the last performance parents hooked up with their kids and drifted out to the parking lot. Dancer walked between her parents, their arms around her, got into their car and drove off.

It was a burden just staring at it, the quarterly Algebra test. Unlike the other subjects, I couldn't draw from memory or logic. By the time the bell rang the majority of questions had gone unanswered. I knew I had not done well. Didn't matter. I had never spoken to Dancer and, after of month of reminders and a week of pleading, Mom had never come to any of the performances. The night I saw Dancer ride away with her parents, I walked home alone.

***

The dream has occured enough times for me to remember. It's not always the same but the theme, vision, or mystery of its tale lingers. It's the house. The house my mother died in. The only house that for a brief time was mine. The house is a darkened maze and it seems as if someone is chasing me through the winding halls and corridors always ending up in the basement where stacks of documents, dusty and ancient, are piled high on top of stuffed metal filing cabinets. I hide behind them.

***

Sugar came out to the picnic table carrying beers. " I'm sorry, " he said, " We didn't know Dartha Vader was coming. I coulda warned you off but the girls woulda been disappointed. " Our eyes drifted to the girls playing with Rums. " That's okay, " I said, " I'll get on her good side yet." We smiled.

It had happened about a year ago. It was an accident. Sugar and I had been out playing pool until the bar closed and I got snockered. He'd forgotten Aunt Blanche was in the spare bedroom. In the darkness I thought the girls had left one of their dolls on the bed. I nonchalantly put my arm around it when the head suddenly turned in my direction. Hair in curlers, face lathered with cream, highlighted by whiskers, and, in the darkness, framing coal black eyes. I started screaming. She started screaming.

The lights came on. Sugar, Candy, and the kids were gaping from the doorway. Not missing a beat Candy said," Weel, Ah see you two have met." I ended up laughing with the faces in the doorway as Aunt Blanche ordered us out. I had suffered her merciless indignation ever since.

" Cherries' comin back from Vegas." Said Sugar. I glanced at Fancy. " That's what I hear.... in time for the fall league?" I said. Sugar nodded.

The girls came and sat down on the grass in front of us. As I gazed down their wings came into view. Though both were mirror images in size and shape there were subtle differences in hues. The blue in Ruby's wings seemed a shade darker, the orange in Opal's brighter. It dawned on me that though Ruby was usually first to talk, Opal had the edge in grades.

Sugar rolled his eyes as Ruby said," You need to get back in bed with Aunt Blanche." Sucking wind to prevent unorthodox language, and noticing Fancy's hand over her mouth I said, " Why's that? " And blurting with passion Opal said," Cause she makes us rub her feet and they smeeall!"

Sugar grabbed his ribs in restraint while Fancy rose to study Candy's roses by the fence. Both offered no guidance as I struggled to respond to precocious ten year olds. About to respond, thank God, I heard Candy say from the back door," Deeners Up Yu Raascalls".

***

I was grounded. I could hear them talking about me in the living room. Eventually Mom said," Bobby, come out here." There was a chair set in the middle of the living room. " Well boyee, what are we gonna do with you?" said Herman," I just don't understand.", shaking his red cheeked face in a sarcastic manner.

It had been a week since we made the drive to school. They went into the Principle's office while I sat outside. It was eerie being there after school was out. The silence grew. I suppose I knew I was going to get caught but I had to take the chance, it had been my first failing grade in anything. The moment I opened the report card and saw that red E beside Algebra, the world seemed awfully small. I took a black pen and turned the E into a B.

" I've been talking to a lawyer." Said Mom, " He tells me that the money Aunt Nanny left you can be used for a private school.... He highly recommended this military academy." She then handed me a brochure. Charlotte Hall Military Academy. There were pictures of cadets in battalion formation, walking to classes with books in their arms, playing sports. " What do you think?"She said, looking at me. " Looks okay to me." I said. Actually it looked great but I didn't want to seem too eager. " There's one thing though," she said, " In order to have the money released, we have to make you legal. Your father and I weren't legally married. Herman needs to adopt you. Is that okay?". I said, " Sure." " In that case," she said, " I'll make the arrangements for you to start this fall. But for the rest of this year you better goddam pass Algebra or I'll beat you to within an inch of your life."

A few days passed, and I was sitting at the table doing homework. Mom looked up from her crosswords and said," You know, you can pick your own middle name if you want to. You've never had one and..... well, I know you loved Earl."

On March 27, 1968, at the age of 13, I became Robert Earl Kenney.

***

" This is the ultimate fact which we so quickly reach on this, as on every topic, the resolution of all into the ever-blessed ONE. Self-existence is the attribute of the Supreme Cause, and it constitutes the measure of good by the degree in which it enters into all lower forms. All things real are so by so much virtue as they contain. Commerce, husbandry, hunting, whaling, war, eloquence, personal weight, are somewhat, and engage my respect as examples of its presence and impure action. I see the same law working in nature for conservation and growth. Power is in nature the essential measure of right. Nature suffers nothing to remain in its kingdoms which cannot help itself. The generation and maturation of a planet, its poise and orbit, the bended tree recovering itself from the strong wind, the vital resources of every animal and vegetable, are demonstrations of the self-sufficing, and therefore self-relying soul. "

From Ralph Waldo Emerson's ' Self-Reliance'.

***

0800

" COMMENCE SHIPS WORK "

I was sitting filling out forms when Louie popped his head in," Spanky, make sure you give him the complete tour, no gundecking, I want him in the Captains Office at 1300." Spanky nodded. Louie turned to me and said," You'll be working for me."

Check-In Sheet in hand I followed Spanky into the passageway. The empty corridors I had wandered over the weekend were now filled with uniformed purpose. A Sailor knelt at a Fire Station scrubbing the brass nozzle of a hose with a wire brush, another, with sponge, wiped down the bulkhead beyond. Bodies passed. Spanky reached back for my sheet and said," If you're working for Louie we better do this right."

It seemed like a whirlwind. Sickbay, Engineering, Ops, and the Post Office, unerringly located by my guide, left me confused and dazed by the ship's maze. Required signatures and brief lectures absorbed the time. Satisfied with our progress it was mentioned that new check-ins had head of line priviledges for chow, with escort of course.

Having dined over the weekend I knew what to expect. At first the most remarkable aspect was a small group of sailors who always sat in a corner and, when the table was full, bowed their heads in silent prayer. With repeated trips the most remarkable was how unremarkable the fare. Roast Beef, Meatballs with noodles, Roast Beef, Spaghetti, Roast Beef. I would soon pray for a home cooked meal.

" MESS GEAR, CLEAR THE MESS DECKS, EARLY DINNER FOR COOKS, MESSCOOKS, AND THE ONCOMING WATCH."

***

It was the last day of school. Days earlier we had all recieved our report cards to present to our parents, get signatures, and hand them back in to our core teachers. I had managed to end the year with a C minus in Algebra. This day was an opportunity for the teachers to say goodbye for the summer.

After lunch we filed into Mrs. Nair's class, excited over the impending release. Some of the girls giggled and the guys looked at each other when she walked in. Instead of the usual slacks and long sleeved shirt, she was dressed in a sleeveless, knee high, brown dress with stockings and high heel shoes. But it wasn't the change of apparel that dismayed us. One could see tufts of hair poking out from her armpits. And when she strolled to the front of the desk, you could see short hairy legs wrapped in nylon. A frightening sight.

"Well class," she said," instead of talking about the last year, I thought we might think about the future." With that she began to write on the blackboard several occupations such as 'Politician', 'Actor/Actress', 'Doctor', 'Lawyer', 'Architect'. With each, the class voted on who would be most likely to become one. For the final category the nominees were told to stand in the hallway while the class voted. When I and the other three were motioned to come back in Mrs.Nair put on a big ceremony about how much she had thoroughly enjoyed us and that she was going back to Europe. Just before the bell rang she announced the winner. It was me. I was voted 'Most likely to Succeed'.

***

Summertime. Riding bikes with the guys, working at the cab co., and hanging out at the apartment pool with furtive glances at the girls. Some days I would go on long walks, generally following a small creek through the neighborhoods. I knew where I could find crawdads and preying mantis', where the red rats and the gray rats lived. I revelled in Nature. And, in accordance with Aunt Nanny's wishes, every Sunday Mom would dress me up in a bow tie and send me to Sunday School and Church.

One Sunday morning Mom gave me a present. It was a white Bible that zippered up on the sides. The front was monogrammed with my new, and legal name, R. Kenney. It's a special feeling going to church with your own Bible. Despite being left on my own, I never skipped. I believed in God.

It was a beautiful day. I was strolling, once again, through the neighborhoods. Filled with emotion, happiness, and optimism, I thought of God, life, and the future. I said to myself," FUTURE ME, LISTEN UP, remember this day. Remember this beauty and splendor. I hope I will be as optimistic in the future as I am now. I hope I will love life as much when I am older whatever my destiny."

Destiny.

***

Scholasticism

"The philosophic and theological movement that attempted to use natural human reason, in particular, the philosophy and science of Aristotle, to understand the supernatural content of Christian revelation."

Equal to when Xerxes was defeated by the Greeks in 480 B.C., to the publication of Galileo's <u>Sidereus Nuncius</u>, and Darwin's <u>Origin of the Species</u>, to projecting the course of western history, cosmology, and thought, may have happened during the year 529A.D.. It was then that the Christian Emperor Justinian closed the doors of the Platonic Academy in Athens and created the "Downfall of the physical establishments of pagan philosophy." That same year Scholasticism was born in the form of the establishment of the first Benedictine Abbey at Monte Cassino.

Considered the "First Scholastic", born in Rome and educated in Athens, a 6th century scholar by the name of Boethius set the standards. While awaiting execution by King Theodoric of Goth for treason, he wrote *The Consolation of Philosophy*, which, aside from the Bible, became one of the most translated and printed books in history. His stated goal, unfinished, was to translate and comment upon,"every book of Aristotle and all the dialogues of Plato."But his fame as a founder of Scholasticism comes from one of his other works wherein he writes an injunction which is adhered to for centuries," As far as you are able, join faith to reason.

This set in motion an unprecedented process of learning for several centuries. The stated goal was to learn, acquire, and preserve the riches of tradition, always reconciling such knowledge with the Christian faith. They maintained that because God was both knowledge and truth he could not contradict himself. They also believed that revelation was the direct teaching of God and held more certainty than natural reason. Therefore, whenever there was a conflict between faith and philosophy, faith was always superior.

A Scholasticism matured, it began to be institutionalized in the universities. At the same time this was happening, the main works of Aristotle, previously unknown, were translated into latin. *Metaphysics, Physics, Nichomachean Ethics,* and *On the Soul* burst onto the scene, electrifying the entire foundation of Christianity. Since these works were by Aristotle, they could not be ignored. His other works, translated with commentaries by Boethius, had been a cultural foundation for centuries. These new works needed, despite the eagerness to assimilate, be balanced with the traditional view and doctrine that had been accepted for centuries. But there was one problem, these books did not come alone, they arrived with Arabic commentators and their heterodox interpretations

The first to accept the challenge of the new Aristotle was a 13th century Dominican, Albertus Magnus. Without knowing Greek he managed to make accessible to the latin west the complete works through commentaries and paraphrases. He was not a scholar in the strictest sense. Like Aristotle, his strength came in the form of direct observation of nature and experimentation. He leaned toward those things in the physical world and managed to record two massive volumes on plants and animals. He even provided new and revolutionary methodological principles saying,"There can be no philosophy without concrete things," and, " in such matters only experience can provide certainty." For Magnus, reconciling faith with reason became more difficult. The problem of integrating all the new knowledge that was amassing would have to be assimilated. That became the task of his pupil, Thomas Aquinas

The most famous intellectual figure of the medieval period was St. Thomas Aquinas. He combined Aristotelian science and Augustinian theology into a comprehensive system of thought that became the authoritative philosophy of the Roman Catholic Church. He wrote on every known subject in philosophy and science and his major works, *Summa Theologica* and *Summa Contra Gentiles* still exert a powerful influence on western thought

Aquinas argued against the Averroists that the truths of faith and the truths of reason cannot conflict but apply to different realms. The truths of natural science and philosophy are discovered by the reasoning of facts and experience, but the tenets of religion, the doctrine of the Trinity, the creation of the world, and Christian dogma are beyond rational comprehension, and though not consistent with reason, must be accepted on faith

Aquinas did not bridge the gap between faith and reason. In answer to his philosophy, and possibly heralding a new outlook for humankind, came two critics, both Franciscans, John Duns Scotus and William of Ockham.

Scotus rejected the reconciliation of rational philosophy with revealed religion. He accepted, in modified version, the Averroists, that religious beliefs are a matter of faith. Ironically, due to the fanaticism of his followers, the word Duns became a derisive term for stupidity in the English language. Dunce.

The English Scholastic William of Ockham maintained that abstract entities are references of words to other words rather than to actual things. The famous rule known as Ockham's razor, where one should not assume the existence of more things than are logically necessary, became a fundamental principle of modern science and philosophy.

Science without Religion is lame. Religion without Science is blind.- Albert Einstein

***

Fall 1968

I started 9th grade wearing a uniform. Black polished shoes, green pants with black stripes down the sides, black belt and silver buckle, khaki shirt with black tie tucked in at the second button, and green cloth hat when, worn properly, lengthwise, topped off the military ensemble.

The chaos of moving in and getting settled ended after the first week, it was a military school after all, and besides, most of the students were returnees. Many were rich kids whose parents despised public education, or feared it. There were a few whose attendance was a legacy. For some it was dictated because public schools wouldn't have them. But for me, I wanted to be there. I knew I needed stability.

Daily routine started with revielle at 0600 sharp. Breakfast would be served from 0615 until 0700. Battalion formation at 0715, where Company Commanders would report to the Battalion Commander, " All present and accounted for sir!", with a sharp salute. After instructions from the BC, the CC's would pass down any additional orders and we would be dismissed, saluting smartly. Classes began at 0730. Unfortunately for me, since there were no classes on the weekends, and attendance was depleted, the same scenario was implemented, wherein I was caught several times skipping muster.

The teachers were all men, and though civilians in civilian clothes, were referred to as Captain. Single Captains took quarters in the barracks, one to each floor. Married Captains occupied housing situated close to the school. The Captains were all eminently qualified, and took personal time toward educating their wards. Their attentions were mostly reciprocated since the Captains had an additional tool of motivation at their disposal, Corporal Punishment on the spot. But in general that tool was used sparingly and judiciously, and only on the most recalcitrant.

Discipline, the hallmark of a military academy. Hours of marching in step, Personnel and Room Inspections. Nurturing responsibility with knowledge.

The Major was the Headmaster of the school. Large as a nose tackle, neck like a bulldog, and, with his crewcut, presented an intimidating figure. For those lucky enough to be in his class dared not doze off, skip an assignment, or display any act of defiance. His subject? Algebra. Oh God.

One day the Major was writing formula's on the blackboard. This kid, a known troublemaker whom I'd had the pleasure of tackling on the football field, was making faces at him behind his back. When another giggled the Major suddenly turned and saw him. With amazing speed the Major stormed toward him and literally lifted him from his desk by the hair and slapped the puppy chow out of both cheeks. Jamming him back into his seat, he then grabbed him by the throat and squeezed asking," Are you making fun of me?" Face red from the slaps and getting redder from the strangulation, the kid, eyes bulging, hands grasping the Major's wrist, frantically tried to shake his head no. The Major released him. For the rest of the year the Major had no problems with him. Me neither.

Throughout the entire year I managed a 96% in Ancient History. The Captain was a tall, dark haired man with a heavy beard. He was unbelievably dull. In his mellow voice he would take the class through the chapters while the others groaned in agony. I was mesmerized. I don't know what the motivation was but I was singularly interested. After the first couple of months, my classmates began to look at me in awe. By the end of the year, in order for my fraternity brothers to pass, I was convinced to sit in an advantageous seat and, for those questions of multiple choice only, hold my pencil north for A, east for B, south for C, west for D, and straight up for E.

***

"We are the eyes of the Universe"
Pico Mirandola, 15th C.

Fall. I have always loved fall. I sense a dramatic inexorable change in the world. Watching the leaves turn, sensing change through the cooler wind upon my cheeks. The sun's earlier exit over the horizon and late rising. There is a visceral feeling of life for me. Where springtime is a beginning for others, Autumn is mine. I suppose it is the trees, the deciduous ones, and how they would shed their splendor, reach naked limbs to the sky to suffer a long winters night, and, in time, live again.

Bundled to the cold I beelined to the campus mini-mart, purchased my daily hot tea, and strode towards my next class. It was another one of those requisite classes in which I felt no motivation but determined to fulfill an older man's dream. And yet I saw the need to infuse a concept of Western Civilization, especially to youth. I saw in the eyes of others, youth all, there was a dearth of knowledge about their origins and history. There were things that high school hadn't covered or if it had needed to be said again.

I took my usual seat in the ampitheatre on the outer row six seats from the front on the speakers left. As the din of arriving students subsided I remembered that we were to have a guest speaker for the day's lecture.

A tall man, he approached the podium with authority. Penny loafers, pressed blue jeans, and corduroy jacket suggested an academic background. But his hair was a hastily combed mess and with glasses thicker than hockey pucks he peered into the audience like a scared owl. But his voice, powered by thought, stilled the room with passion and energy. He said:

'In order to better understand how Scholasticism became so execrable to some, and how Humanism arrived on the world scene, one must review the philosophies of the ancients.'

'Pre-Socratic Greece, 6th to 5th century B.C., is fundamental to Plato's and Aristotle's philosophies. Many of these thinkers lived in outlying colonies and contributed to concepts such as Socrates process of Critical Inquiry. They asked such questions as, "What is there in the natural world? What is fundamental reality? How do we account for change? The seasons? The fluxing of the material world? What are the fundamental elements?"Such men as Thales, Anaximander, and Anaximenes provided much in this early measure of the universe.'

'The Pre-Socratics developed the process of logic through reasoning, discovery, argument, and debate. They provided the foundation for the two major concepts necessary to modern science, Dialectic thought and Falsification. Dialectic thought being when someone has an idea, a thesis, another gives an antithesis, and from both comes a synthesis, which in itself is a thesis, and once again comes an antithesis. Believing that nothing advances without contradiction. Falsification is when in a debate, the argument is capable of being proved wrong. Or in other words, divine acts are incapable of being proved wrong. Hence the genesis of scientific thought, that which is testable and capable of being proven or disproven.

'Plato, 427-347 B.C., supported a predesigned universe. Living during a chaotic century with the Persian and Peloponesian wars, it was still a time for creativity. A student of Socrates, he ponders what is the fundamental reality. He begins the concept of epistemology- the study of the theory of knowledge. He believes that when we talk of reality we speak of something that is perfect. He defines that which is perfect is unchanging. Reality is made up of concept, form, or idea. It is another world of the soul which is trapped in the body. He is skeptical of the senses and empirical reality. He agrees with the Pythagoreans that mental concept is reality, that forms exist out of time. It is the reality of ideas that is important, only the ideal realm makes the physical happen. In an analogy written in the work "Republic", Plato depicts people as being chained inside a cave and observe their world as shadows upon the wall. He defines true philosophers as those who see where the shapes come from, outside the cave and in the light.'

'But if ideas and forms exist outside of space and time, and redemption of the soul requires denying the physical, then ideas are fixed concepts. If that is the case, then how do things change?

'In his book "Timaeus", Plato describes his conceptual theory of matter to account for change. And after describing his fundamental stuff, he challenges others to prove him wrong. In true dialectic fashion, his most famous student, Aristotle, does not agree at all.

'If one concept is held by both Plato and Aristotle, it is that each assumes a pre-existing order to the universe. But unlike Plato, Aristotle believes that matter and form are simply mental categories, not an ontological being. The names of things does not mean other realms. He does not belive in souls. He is a materialist who embraces the senses.

'Aristotle might also be called Mr. Teliology, the study of anything in terms of purpose, goal, or endpoint. To him change is the same as motion and life is a form of motion. When change accomplishes its goal, it is at rest.'

'Even here, between the giants of antiquity, one can see the chasm between faith and reason.....'

The class ended. I donned jacket and backpack entranced, and strode towards the exit. Stepping into the brisk autumn air the Sun, bundled by clouds for days, pierced its cover and illuminated the courtyard with recrudescent splendor. Sunshine.

***

Spring 1969

It was a three day weekend. Peter and Wally came out to pick me up. Not so much because I would be virtually alone at the school, but because Peter needed help moving.

I could sense jealousy. I was the MaMa's boy, spoiled and tender. They referred to me as " the little bastard" and addressed me as "Boyee". Being naive I never took offense, I was surprised to have brothers.

The drive back was harrowing. Speeding over 80 through rural Maryland ,Wally, while driving, took the occasion to shoot at road signs while Peter kept stabbing him in the ribs with a military issue knife. My asshole ripped several holes in the back seat. By the time we got back to civilization it was too late to start moving, so we briefly stopped by to say high to Mom and Pop, made arrangements for me to spend the weekend with the boys, and lit out.

We toured the suburbs. Peter and Wally steadily polishing off beers. It was dark when they decided to pull the stuff out. Wally and Peter had been in the Marines, Peter had been kicked out. The reason was because Peter and Wally had raided the armory. Wally had had the keys but Peter had taken credit for it and got kicked out. It was about nine thirty driving through Queenstown, that citizens watched flares go up in the sky and motorists found themselves driving amidst smoke bombs.

" So Boyee, you got a boyfriend at that school?" Said Wally.

" Yeah, I bet he's got a lot of boyfriends." Said Peter.

" Yeah, he's gonna be a faggot when he grows up." Said Wally.

Sex was a big thing with these guys.

***

A Night to Remember

After my first hitch in the Navy, I traversed the country about three times, and briefly settled in Reno to live with my Dad for a few months. At that time he was separated from my stepmother and we both got a room on the outskirts of town. It was a horseshoe shaped motel with one end the office and the other a small bar. I forget the name of both, but not one particular night.

One day my Dad and I went into this bar for the first time. Small place. Maybe 14 seats at the counter with a couple of tables against the wall. The owner, who served the drinks and lived upstairs, was a slight late thirties kinda guy who seemed especially polite and meticulous. After a few minutes, our eyes adjusted to the artificial darkness, we noticed the other patrons as well as some of the posters and paraphernalia.

On the walls were posters of men dressed in black leather with silver studs. The other patrons, dressed in pastels and exuding an aura of femininity, regarded us as a couple and soon entered into animated conversation. Calling each other "Bitch" and "Slut" and discussing their most recent acquisition. My Dad and I quickly finished our drinks and left. From the moment we left the front door until the time we arrived at the room, about 50 yards, we were doubled over in laughter. He never went in there again

One night I was bar hopping. Playing pool. Being the foolish young man. It was o"dark thirty when I arrived at the motel, and, seeing the lights of another bar, decided to go in. The owner, who by now knew me and my Dad as well as my sexual orientation, served me a drink at the end of the bar and returned to his compadres

Suddenly, a huge figure entered the bar screaming,"Who's been messing with my kid?" I immediately placed him as the boyfriend of the girl I had been hitting on who lived a few doors down. Never met him."Which one of you faggots messed with the kid?" The kid wasn't his. But it turned out that the little boy had been throwing rocks at the cars in the parking lot earlier in the day and one of the gentelladies came out and said,"Cut it out, you little cum drop.

The owner, as well as his customers, was terrified. He proceeded down the bar challenging each person like a Goliath. When he got to me, pie-eyed to the gills and filled with youthful vigor, I said,"Let's go outside, you big ...."

Duh! He was big and obviously a bad buckaroo. But believe it or not, even more soused than me. We stepped outside the front door and squared off. I managed to evade the haymakers, but had to leap to hit him in the face. Miraculously, I knocked him down three times, but he kept getting up. All the while, the owner and his customers watched from the front door.

After the third leap, I landed awkwardly on my right foot. Sprained it. He was down and I decided to finish my drink. I limped my way back to my seat

I thought the night had been quite filling, but the villiage idiot decided to come back for more. As I sat there, I saw 8 to 10 homosexuals converge on this gentlema... no not gentleman, fool, and saw the most hair pulling, kicking, and penultimate asskickicking of my adult life

The next day he was picked up for warrants by the Police. I also found out that he had been the Light Heavyweight Champ of his Marine Division. I never saw his girlfriend again. Unrequited love. Story of my life

***

She was taller than I by a few inches. We were an uncommon union. But our thoughts and beliefs, revealed in trust, created a union we both knew was unique. I knew she was someone, someone special. The moments between conversations were filled with mutual thoughts, and, mutual loyalty. We didn't dance well together, we were awkward walking down the street together, but those things don't matter for young minds in love. Most first loves are blind. In the ecstasy of finding a soul mate the physical is subsumed by the living concious thought that one has a partner in life.

***

Summer, 1969

I marched proudly during graduation ceremonies. Mom and Pop were in the stands. Instructors had given my mother glowing remarks despite the fact that I had recieved considerable demerits. She was beaming. I was elated.

Though I felt I had made accomplishments it was clear, once back on the homestead, that things hadn't changed all that much. I knew the routine and settled in. Hanging out at the pool, the guys, working at the Cab Co., strolling the neighborhoods. I tried to stay out as late as possible in order to miss the nightly squabbles.

One night I came in a little too early. They were at it again. I could measure the intensity by the strength of hand shuffling, bloodshot eyes, and, on this evening, drool.

" GODDAMMIT, I DON'T WANNA HEAH NO MOOOOR." Severe rocking. hands shuffling, spittle spewing with each T, drool pooling at the end of his chin.

" GODAMMIT, YOU'RE GONNA HEAR IT.... IF I CATCH YOU WITH THAT FUKIN WOMAN, MUCH LESS GOIN TO THE RACETRACK WITH HER, I SWEAR TO GOD YULE PAY.' Shaking her finger, cheeks red.

I said." Don't you two ever stop, PLEEEEESE, the whole world can hear you."

"BOYEEE, DON'T FUK WITH MEEEE, DON'T THINK YOU'RE TOO BIG FOR THE BELT." With that he reached under the seat again to pull out the belt, and once again a pack of L&M's came with it. OOPS!

Once pledged to a fraternity, and accepted, the Pledge is required to follow all the whims of fellow fratmates during what's called a Hell Week and then a Hell Night. Throughout the week I raised my happy ass early to warm toilet seats for the seniors, shined shoes and belt buckles, ran errands and carried books. Hell night required attacks upon the other frats, filling lists such as snagging a jock strap from another CC, soaping their frat houses, and eating a concoction specially cooked up for the occasion. And in the Key house, some members made us smoke cigarettes. By the time the year ended, I was a regular smoker, being our frat house was removed from the campus and not regularly visited, we got away with it.

" WELL, BOYEE, WHAT THE FUK IS THIS?" Says Herman.

" Goddammit Bobby, I thought we taught you a lesson." Said Mom

Silence. Guilty. Did it again, Dummy.

" Have a seat BOYEE," He said, handing me another Blunt. The belt between us.

He pulled out his gold lighter and lit er up. I pulled deeply. Not used to cigars I momentarily coughed bringing a smile to Mom's face. Then I pulled again and started to make smoke rings and french inhaling through the nose. Mom's face assumed a livid rictus of anger and suddenly exploded," GIMME THAT FUKIN BELT." Reaching between me and Herman. Herman grabbed the belt with his right hand, held her back with his left and, for the first time he was ever cool towards me said:

" LET THE MAN ENJOY HIS SEEGARR, GLADEESE, LET THE MAN ENJOY HIS SEEGARR."

This was the second time I smoked a cigar. It was assumed that I was going to smoke, but from then on I couldn't have any of Mom's cigarettes and had to buy my own. And, of course, I couldn't smoke in the house.

***

We all sat down at the kitchen table, Sugar at one end, Blanche at the other. I sat between the twins facing Fancy and Candy's spot. Candy passed out bowls as I grabbed the girls knees for giggles. Blanche gave us a stern look.

Candy took her seat beside Fancy and said," Deeeg inn". Blanche began tapping her nails on the table and said," Shouldn't we be saying Grace?", eyeing the twins. Candy nodded at the girls and, in stereo, they said," Father we thank thee for the food and drink which lays before us, Bless the hands that prepared it, and forgive us for Christ's sake, Amen."

Opal poked me in the ribs as I ladled Georgia Stew into Ruby's bowl. Caught offguard I spilled, jumped, and forced Ruby to drop her spoon on the floor. Under Blanche's menacing gaze I quickly bent and rose towards the kitchen to wash it off. From the kitchen sink I could see her wings.

They seemed small, stiff, and unmoving. Basic gray with sharp streaks of an angry red reaching to the tips. Yet the tips were laced with flecks of a bluish gold and as I turned back to the table I noticed a soft pink hidden deep in the stems. I said." Aunt Blanche, may I bring you some more wine?" She nodded.

She lifted her finger to motion enough. As I muscled the cork back I said, in front of the whole family," I'm very sorry about what happened last year, please forgive me." I could tell I had caught her off guard. Her face briefly flushed. Her eyes met mine

93

with an unusual kindness, brief yet piercing, and then she said," Eat your stew." A small smile on her lips.

Candy was pleased. " So y'all gonna be a team again when Cherrie gets back..... Be nice to see a fourth first place trophy over the stage at Smitty's." Sugar looked proud, Fancy confident. I said," Let's see if she's kept her game up."

"Yu know, my Henry never had time for things like playing pool." All eyes stretched towards Blanche. Accepting the spotlight she continued," We had to scrimp to make ends meet... Yo Mama (looking at Candy) never wanted cuz I saw to it my little sister wouldna need for...but I guess... she'da been proud of ya now." Candy beamed.

Silence followed. Through the window I saw a Robin land on a tree limb. I heard it call to its mate in the dusk. I wondered where they had their nest. I felt the twins bending to their spoons, Sugar tipping his beer, Candy napping her lips, and the warmth of Fancie's gaze. And I felt, saw, and heard Blanche's face drop into the remnants of her Georgia stew. Her wings were gone.

The coroner said it was a massive cardiac. Immediate and untreatable. But I still see that Robin, wings spread in urgency, singing to his mate.

***

Bury me someplace barren. Where the sun the only warmth, the wind the only sound, the moon and stars the only audience. Where only toughened grass springs from caked earth and starving trees the only shade. That's life enough for me. I don't want my ashes spread over some exotic spot, I wish to dissolve wholly into the planet that made me. Make me not a member of a dead zoo, where the exhibits pay to enter and be forgotten. Shroud me in a burlap bag and within ceremony cover me with silence. Bury me where some future traveler might tred and sense the wonder of the world with mindful eye, and, unknowingly, be my passport to the future.

***

Fall 1969

My roomate and I had been invited over to the Teak House. Both of us now Buck Sergeants and returning veterans we were challengers to other frats over future dominance of the school and influence over prospective inductees. It was a friendly invitation, despite affiliations, we were all friends and classmates.

The Teak House was carved out of abandoned rooms underneath the cafeteria. Our sponsor led us down a flight of steps, along a darkened passageway, turned left, and opened a freshly painted door with their logo on it. We entered.

It was a wide room with several couches, polished tile floor, and teak walls. There were five other sophomores lounging with one Junior sitting in the corner. Our sponsor led us to the middle of the room and said," I believe you know these guys.". We looked around and smiled. I pointed to an academic adversary who happened to have been our freshman class president the previous year and said," YOU!", in mock anger. It was then that Junior said," NOW."

Junior. One of the biggest guys on campus. Lineman on the football team. Staff sergeant. Always using his weight to get his way but put down by the Senior's who were all Officers. He was really a nice guy, kind of a big puppy, but prone to asserting his size.

The lights went out. My roomate and I were suddenly assaulted from all sides by a massive pillow fight. Laughing we snagged pillows in the dark and swung back. Out numbered we found ourselves huddled in the middle of the floor when the lights came back on, Junior on top of us.

Our fellow sophomores saw the situation. The lights went back out. From underneath Junior's massive weight we felt him being pummeled. In darkness we slipped out from under him and joined the concerted attack until he cried," Stop,Stop, Okay,Okay."

Fact is Junior and I liked each other, but there was a time when he caused me pain.

***

He was a new Captain, young, recently graduated from college. A big fellow, more like a gorilla, who had gained laurels in sports from his home state. He was open and friendly which was not in keeping with the staid and stiff composures of his colleagues. Though all were friendly in their own way, he became more like one of the guys. This backfired.

As the year progressed cadets became more boisterous and obstreperous in his classroom. Eventually, reports from other Captains to the Major caused a major change in behavior. With great fanfare and stern warnings the Captain produced a large wooden paddle the size of a tennis racket. It had whiffle holes bored in it to assist in impact. Making no doubts about it, he was willing to, for the undisciplined cadet, carve the first name on the handle of he who didn't believe him.

Biology was the subject and I had studied long and hard the night before. The exam would be on the classifications of the animal kingdom. I was sure I'd do well.

We filed silently into the classroom. The Captain was sitting at his desk reading. The heretofore unused paddle propped in the corner. I took a seat in the middle of the classroom. Junior sat right behind me.

Without any sense of humor on his face the Captain began handing out the exams. He said," I want to hear complete silence during this test." He took his seat and began reading. I placed my name at the top of the sheet and began answering the questions.

After a couple of minutes I felt something touching the back of my left ear. I brushed it off. Something again tickling my ear. Suddenly I knew it was Junior playing with his pencil. Without thought I turned quickly and glared at him. The movement caught the Captain's eye.

" KENNEY ", The Captain barked.

"Yes Sir."

" Didn't I say I wanted complete silence?"

" Yes Sir ."

" Come up here. "

I rose from my seat, looked at Junior, and stepped to the front of the class. He already had the paddle in his hand. " Face the door and put your hands to your knees.", he said. I obeyed. He braced himself and took a two handed grip. There was a sudden whoosh then... WHAP!!!

The wave of pain caused me to stand straight up on my toes. Hands clenched, teeth locked, I managed to shuffle to the corner and stand there shielding my tears from the others. Moments passed. Suppressing tears I turned and returned to my seat. Junior's face was red with guilt. I heard him whisper," I'm sorry."

When the period ended I moved quickly to the door. From the corner of my eye I saw one of the CC's, who had seen the whole thing, rush to the Captains desk and began whispering in his ear.

I sat in the back of the class for the rest of the year.

***

What is a primate? In order to answer that question, one must recognize where the word "Primate" came from. In 1758, Linnaeus, in composing his taxonomy of the world's organisms, used this term to describe that order of mammals that included the monkeys, apes, and humans. Primate comes from the latin word *primas,* meaning "of the first rank", putting humans as first among the animals. There were two types of primates, the prosimians (Latin for "before monkeys") and anthropoids (Greek for "human-like"). In order to be included within the taxonomy of primates, species must have shared certain characteristics (Boaz p.173)

It is estimated that the "Age of Mammals" began with a common ancestor around 55 million years ago. Since then primates have evolved ranging from as small as the mouse lemur to as great as an extinct ape as tall as 12 feet (Park p.109). Of 200 extant species and as many as 6000 extinct, some but not all of the following characteristics are shared among them

- nails instead of claws at the end of digits

- divergent (opposable) thumb and big toe

- forward orientation of the eye sockets (stereoscopic vision)

- large to very large brain size relative to the body

- a generalized dentition (Wolpoff p.73)

In these suite of elements that are mostly shared by primates, there are certain features that are shared by other species not associated with primates yet give rise as to how our earliest ancestors may have adapted to their niche. There are two hypotheses theorizing how the earliest primates may have adapted these characteristics, the arboreal and visual predation.

Primates have a wide range of locomotion ranging from vertical clinging and jumping, brachiation, knuckle walking, and bipedalism. These modes appear evolutionary in that order. The Arboreal Hypothesis argues an adaptation to life in the trees, stipulating that grasping hands and feet were superior adaptations, thus requiring acute vision (it may have also set the stage for reproduction, brain growth, and a generalized skeleton). Using the comparative approach, Cartmill opposed this theory with the Visual Predation hypothesis. He used distinctive elements of primate characteristics and compared them with other species. His results state that primate characteristics are adaptations by a small arboreal mammal in stalking insect prey, captured in the hands (Lewin 128/9). Both theories support the concept of arboreality, where for millions of years these traits were strengthened, adapted, and formed the base traits now shared by all primates

When Linneaus devised his taxonomic system, 101 years before Darwin's "Origin of Species", his primary purpose was to name all God's creatures. He was a creationist. Yet like Ptolemy and Galileo he was skilled and adept in his scientific observations. Classifying living organisms according to similarities and differences (Park p.105), his system has remained valid to this day. But this system was based on the phenotypical appearances of the organisms, not their genetic makeup. Today we can fine tune Linneaus' taxonomic system through actual evolutionary relationships. This system is called *Cladistics* (Park p.109).

Traditionally there has always been three hominoid families, the Hylobatidae (lesser apes), Pongidae (great apes), and Hominidae (humans and their fossil ancestors). Under the new revisionist system of Cladistics there are still 3 families but now with two subfamilies included under Hominidae (Anth 101 notes):

Hylobatidae	Pongidae	Hominidae	
(lesser apes)	(Orangutan)	Paninae	Homininae
(Chimp & Gorilla)		(Human & Ancestors)	

What is a Primate? It appears to be a family of creatures with one common arboreal ancestor whose base traits have evolved into a suite of characteristics common to all. As the archeological record is augmented with new discoveries we can be sure that subtle changes may yet happen to how we define and order our family tree. But now we have a new tool in assessing the branches and the roots, our genes. Much like Linneaus did not have the benefit of Darwin's research, Darwin did not have the benefit of Mendel's. What new paradigm could be next?

***

What comes around, goes around.

It was a couple weeks before graduation ceremonies. We filed into Biology class and I took my usual seat in the back of the classroom. It was the first half of a two part final, the second half to be administered next week as an open book. The Captain started handing out the tests. As they were being handed back some commotion erupted in Junior's area. The CC in the class immediately, as the Captain turned to see, pointed toward Junior.

The Captain motioned Junior to the front of the class. Right in the same spot where I had endured. It almost seemed as if staged. Junior assumed the position. I had a birds eyes view of faded green pants stretched around an enormous ass that was getting larger. The Captain took his baseball stance, aimed, and delivered with thunderous energy. WHAP! I saw the back of his thick neck turn red, and then his ears after he jerked up straight. He quivered in restraint. Somehow I knew there was a sense of justice being felt in the classroom, but for me there was a blankness and feeling of sadness. I couldn't watch. I knew what that paddle, wielded by a large man with a mission, felt like.

Graduation ceremonies came. Once again marching proudly, with Mom and Pop in the stands, I considered this school my second home. A future junior, I expected to fulfill the four year curriculum with honors. I knew I had two families. I wondered why Mom seemed to be overly critical of the school on the way home.

***

The Key Society

Nestled in the rolling hills of rural Maryland, Queen Anne's County, is a place that specialized in the nurturing of young minds and spirits, Charlotte Hall Military Academy. It's closed now, unable to keep up with the forces of society, but for two years it was my universe and in my memories the doors will always be open

I arrived in the fall of 68'. Loaded down with uniforms specially made by a tailor shop in Baltimore, I said my goodbyes to Mom and Pop, located my room on the third floor of the barracks, and settled in

There were four fraternities on campus; the Keys; the Teaks; the Jeffersonians; and the Washingtonians. The last two were the scholars, though to be a member to any group one had to maintain high grades. The Teaks played football. The Keys...Lacross

I tried out for the football team. I was small for my age, still am, but I was determined to play sports as I had in Little League. During tryouts I would have to be tough because most of the others had an edge in size. An early reputation would be important

I recall a tall gangly boy, known as a troublemaker, catching a pass in my area. He would be tough to tackle. A good 6" taller, the word was that of a sadistic bully. Only ten yards away, an eternity, I built up speed and rammed my helmet into his midsection. He fell gasping. As he rose, fear in his eyes, he commented as if I were trying to kill him. Respect.

I was recruited by the Keys because they liked my roomate, and asked to join the Lacross team. I didn't blink. Unlike the other frats, the Keys had a house situated in the woods 100 yards behind the football field. Private and secluded, the Key Society was the best fraternity on campus

I made lifelong friends there. My second year I was Vice President of the Sophomore Class, member of the Drill Team, Lacross Team, and Honor Roll. I also had accumulated 116 demerits for skipping reveille and getting caught taking orders on

101

the third floor, and, after taps, following the railroad tracks to the Chicken Ranch and returning with armloads of hamburgers and chicken. I raked a lot of leaves.

Despite a sizeable scholarship, my family couldn't afford to send me back. I regret that I didn't graduate from there. But the memories and good times linger on in my heart and soul.

***

It was strange when I walked in the door. Mom, Pop, Peter, and Wally were sitting there looking at me. Peter grabbed a chair and placed it in the middle of the living room. He said," Have a seat boyee."

I took a seat facing the "Family". Mom seemed to have a look of guilt, my brothers a look of glee, and Herman a look of defiance. Peter said," You can't go back to that school this year." I said," Why Not?". Mom said," Because there isn't any more money."

Something was wrong. I knew that the yearly costs were no more than 2,500$ a year. It was known that I was being offered a 1,000$ scholarship to return. Even without that the yearly costs wouldn't deprive me of four years if Aunt Nanny had left me 10,000$.

" Well, there just isn't any more money." Said Herman. I looked around. There were no sympathies nor explanations. And I never had to ask for one. I knew what happened.

***

Fall 1970

Public school. Culture Shock. There was a new High School in Largo,MD., straight down Landover Road, past the beltway, down 202, next to a new Community College. Though Largo was considered an upper class neighborhood, buses were delivering students from less priviledged areas. I was one of those. I'd never experienced such animosity. Even in Palmer Park Jr. High, a black neighborhood, most of whose students I was going back to school with, despite childhood rivalries or animosities, such differences in race or color were never magnified, much less attended to with such vigorous zeal and uninhibited violence. What was being taught?

Charlotte Hall had never been like this. If two fellows wanted to square off they could just meet behind the PX. But here fights broke out in the hallways right in front of you. And the reasons were racial animus. Going to school, on a daily basis, was scary. At Charlotte Hall all races, nationalities, and religions were represented. There were no persecutions or hostilities based on differences, we were all the same. All the same and yet different. I wondered, why?

***

The Origin of Modern Humans

One of the most debated issues in paleoanthropology is the origin of modern humans. Two competing hypotheses prevail, multiregionalism and the Out of Africa theories. Did an early ancestor evolve somewhere in east Africa about 1 million years ago and expand into Asia and Europe and develop into modern humans or was there an early exodus of species that was supplanted by anotomically modern humans some 150 to 50 kya? What does the record show? Which concept seems most liable? Will there ever be a complete record that definitively shows our origins

Multiregionalism utilizes a concept known as *regional continuity.* Regional continuity supposes that the diversity and characteristic traits of different geographical regions are due to one species that settled in these areas around 1 million years ago and developed separately. That species, H. erectus, maintained enough gene flow through these isolated populations to ensure viable reproductive success during this time. This theory has also been called the Candelabra hypothesis.

The Out of Africa, and Out of Africa 2, theories contend that an early migration may have taken place 1 mya but anatomically modern humans didn't appear on the scene until about 150 kya in east Africa and expanded from there. It is suggested that diversity and genetic traits within populations were the result of adaptation and genetic drift within the last 100,000 years or so.

These predictions should be confirmed by the fossil record. If Multiregionalism is correct there should be the appearance of AMH remains over a broad swath of the Old World detailing transitional fossils and supporting isolated populations and their emergence into modern humans around the same times. Each region would have a record of these populations, and both anatomically and genetically, each could display their own unique history over such a vast amount of time. On the other hand, if Out of Africa is confirmed, there should be a record of early man

104

throughout the different regions but no transitional manifestations until 150 kya with the emergence of AMH detailed from the regions of east Africa and expanding from there

From the readings I would support the Out of Africa theory. There seems to be no record of modern human behavior until about 150 to 50 kya. There are no transitional specimens spanning the Old World except in the region of east Africa. The record abruptly changes around 50 kya, suggesting the appearance of a new influence in these regions rather than a slow development of indigenous peoples.

What is the most powerful example to me is the disappearance of the Neandertal's. We know that they occupied a large swath of Europe for a great deal of time. Uncontested, they seem to have evolved into a particular niche with varying degrees of success. But they were not anatomically modern. They seem to be the natural growth and development of an earlier migration. Still yet not a population to have developed an innovative culture. Culture, the hallmark of humankind, suddenly appears on the scene about 40 kya. The appearance of a new influence, one innovative and culturally adaptive, now competes for the same resources. In accordance with this shift in the record, the new influence seems to have had a profound effect upon the Neandertal's. They become extinct within 10 kya

The current archeological record supports the Out of Africa predictions. Multiregionalism, despite such notable names as Milford Wolpoff, seems not to answer the fact that currently there is no evidence suggesting transitional forms throughout the various regions. The expansion of a parent population from east Africa around 150 kya seems to allow for the diversity and adaptations that we see today. Gene flow and interaction would maintain reproductive viability and continue genetic compatibility. I feel that further discoveries will support Out of Africa, evidence of transitional forms as well as DNA has continued to support it. Yet one region may not have been the only forge for humankind, should finds suggest another fire somewhere else, the debate will be energized once again.

***

With the pool closed there were few things for us guys to do. We naturally migrated, for relative freedom, to the other half of the hill behind the complex. The Woods. It was not a new thing. We had done it, on and off, for the last two summers. Whenever one had some money, we'd go the the local hardware store and buy a can, a special brand, some bags, and view the natural world through the hallucinations brought on by sniffing industrial glue. There were days when I came home loaded, they never knew.

The Woods was a whole world within itself. We sniffed every part of it. It took on a life and personality all its own. One day we had settled on one side of the hill, where, from our vantage point, we were eye level with the third floor of an adjoining complex.

There were five of us. Seated in a semi-circle, we spread the bags and glue between us. It was a golden day, the sun shining brightly through the leaves, my back to a tree. Time became disjointed. It didn't register at first. The blue uniform approaching through the bushes. It still wasn't real when I saw the sun glinting off his badge. But when he stood in the middle of us and caught the one who tried to flee it became real. We were caught.

All the parents had to come down to the station to pick us up. Each was amazed we were doing such a thing. Since we were all still minors, probation, under the purview of our guardians, was ordered. Our records would be expunged once we turned 18.

***

November 16, 1970

Monday. A school day. The day after my 16th birthday. I had been grounded for over two months. Not even allowed out on my birthday. Listening to the nightly diatribes and comdemnations of my behavior had become onerous. The monies I had "saved " from working at the station, held by Herman, were moot since I wasn't going to get a drivers license even though I had passed Driver's Ed with flying colors. 'I hadn't deserved it'. I knew this was an excuse to not have to pay for insurance even though I had been driving cabs around the block for a couple years to check out their brakes. I felt smothered. I hadn't even recieved many birthday presents, except for a couple of dollars from Mom and a black leather jacket from Dad. I was ready to explode. My very spirit in jeopardy.

I hadn't really made up my mind. But when that son of a bitch threw that cold glass of water in my face that morning, I knew I was going. I dressed heavily and put on my black leather jacket, grabbed my savings, and skipped breakfast. Mom walked me to the door for the kiss goodbye. She didn't know my plans. She had always cared for me. I knew that and loved her deeply for it. We kissed, I took two steps away and turned back for another. I kissed Mom twice that morning.

***

Man and Nature in the Renaissance (pps.1-73)

The Renaissance represents man's spiritual, social, and cultural evolution from the middle ages to enlightenment.. Using the ancients observations and philosophies, science and thought emerged flavored with Platonic, Aristotelian, and Biblical rationalizations and reconcilations. This period of discovery and invention created profound changes, contrasting with traditional thought and religious ideology, forcing new approaches to the physical world and our place in it.

Of the inventions during this period none had more impact than the Printing Press, Gunpowder, and the Magnet. Revolutionizing dissemination of information, warfare, and navigation(p.1). Growth of languages maintained pace with the ability to mass produce the printed word. The formation of a new science caused attempts to unify or reconcile the Aristotelian and Occult(p.13). Mathematics became known as natural magic(p.21). Alchemy, the science, proved valuable to the future science of chemistry, if only for the emphasis of observation and evidence to what is real and can be proved, another new outlook(p.17). The new study of Nature built upon the works of the ancients(p.35), and in turn, provided the foundation for future visionaries, I believe, such as Darwin. Ancient errors to human anatomy and blood flow are corrected(p.57).

This is a fascinating period. To look back and see how individuals and societies coped with, resisted, or changed with these discoveries and schools of thought. As our civilization has had a Renaissance, don't we as individuals have one too where, at some point, with our own accumulated knowledge we choose our personal philosophies, outlooks, and lifestyles and break with or at least reconcile our ancients (i.e.parents)

***

I walked to the new Burger King where, for the last couple of weeks, a friend had been picking me up and taking me to school, saving me the burden of the buses. I explained to him that I was running away. Didn't care where. Then suddenly I asked him if he would give me a ride if I gave him some gas money. Of course it meant that he would miss a day of school, but he was willing. He drove me to Charlotte Hall.

I stayed at the Key House. The guys brought me some food and I debated my future. On the morning of the third day I knew, somehow, that it was time to go. I got up early, left a thank you note, and followed the railroad tracks to the highway. I didn't know that while I was hitch hiking on the highway, the family had sent an emissary to pick me up.

Traffic was light in this part of the state. It occurred to me that picking up a stranger in a black leather jacket was not something I would do. It was only an hour when I turned to thumb an approaching car, a small blue sports car, and was delighted to see that it was a fellow Key, graduated, waving me in.

Some one must have contacted him but he never said so. He was rooming with another graduate at the local college. We went there. We talked and it was decided that I contact my father. I did. He wired me some money and in two days I was on a bus to Reno, Nevada.

***

1300

"COMMENCE SHIPS WORK"

" You'll be working for me in the Captains Office. It's much like the Personnel Office but here we'll be working directly for the Captain, ship's correspondence and stuff like that, you'll see.......and I've arranged with Mulroy, you'll be cleaning the compartment two days a week then back up here every afternoon. Any Questions?... Here, let me see that check-in list."

As he scanned the sheet I scanned the office. Everything seemed meticulous, organized, and inspection ready, right down to the wax buffed floor. This added to an increasing anxiety magnified by Spanky's timid behavior as we climbed the ladderbacks entering Officers Country. He was solemn as he led me past the CO's and XO's Staterooms and delivered me to the office. Spanky, wordlessly, left.

" Don't be intimidated.", Said Louie, " Certainly decorum is more pronounced up here, and you'll bust your ass cleaning and keeping paperwork in order, but, " and he turned his kind and knowing gaze towards me," You make me look good, and I'll make you look good." I suddenly felt like I was part of a team. I nodded, and smiled.

He who is to be a good ruler must have first been ruled. - Aristotle, *Politics*

***

Curiosity of the world, once again, took over. Varied peoples boarded and left, destinations and lives unknown left me wondering. Individualism and a sense of maturity entered my thoughts and being.

I usually sat in the back of the bus, since I was in for the long haul. I had books to read but for the most part my gaze would be out the window. About a third of the way a group of young people, only a couple of years older than I, boarded. They were lively and talkative, joking with complete strangers with familiarity. Long haired, blue jeaned and barefooted, both guys and girls, exhibited their freedoms with complete abandon. I looked up to them. Soon, with some urging, we were singing songs and playing games. My future was brightening.

An older man, sitting towards the front, turned to look at us several times. A look of annoyance on his face. Eventually he said, " Could you all keep it down back there?", then mumbling something about disrespectful youth and why weren't they serving their country. The magic word was then whispered, " Viet Nam".

One of the girls said," Why should we be fighting over there, it doesn't make sense?"

" Because ", the man said, " We're defending freedom from Communism."

A young man with long dark curls, headband with peace sign, and faded army jacket leaned forward and said," It's not our war, all we're doing is throwing lives away.... give us something to fight for."

"You kids don't know what it's like to fight for something."said the man," America, love it or leave it... I DID MY TIME IN THE BIG ONE... I DID MY TIME." Stretching his leg across the aisle, pulling his pants leg up, and showing a livid, jagged scar from ankle to kneecap.

The young man said," I DID MY TIME TOO!", lifting his right arm over the aisle. A prosthetic hand attached with the middle finger sticking out.

The argument was over and silence filled the bus. After awhile the young lady sitting beside me said," It's all so wrong... the military machine is running everything.What do you think?" I thought for a moment," It does seem wrong." I neglected to mention Charlotte Hall.

By the time I reached Reno, I had a sense of purpose, if not an understanding of the world. I knew there was good and evil, right and wrong, but now there seemed to be shadings and levels in which only ones education and personal experiences would decide. It was an Age of Discovery.

It was during the silent times that I constructed a poem to support an Age of Discovery:

An aborted child, the human waste
May yet be better than one born in haste
If it is our will to create human breath
Is it for fun or to lessen our death?
Yet should this one rise, rise above the riff raff
Clap to that Bastard, he has the last laugh

***

Marco Polo's <u>The Travels</u> and Bernal Diaz' <u>The Conquest of New Spain</u>: a Contrast and Comparison

These two remarkable works are enlightening not only for their time but for today's as well, giving insight and personal perceptions of peoples, cultures, and customs that historians can refer to for centuries to come. Though these are stories of adventure, one in Asia and the other the America's, one author Spanish and the other Italian, and both separated by over two centuries, they both have common threads. Through the authors perceptions of western thought, one can envision exotic cultures, cosmology, great battles, and immense wealth. Both have paralells and ironies, famous figures, and fortuitous events that spice the fabric of history and color our view of the "Age of Discovery"

These books might not have been written. Marco Polo's <u>The Travel's</u> was a collaboration with a professional romance writer, Rustichello of Pisa, while both were prisoners of war in Genoa(MP p.17), six years after his return from the orient. Meticulous details of cities, customs, cosmology, food, flora, fauna, and the Mongol Empire by an observant merchant is flavored in the romantic tradition and presented with a western viewpoint. This book was one of five in Cristopher Columbus' library. It was heavily annotated and must have had direct impact on his decision to seek the East Indies in 1492.

1492 was also the year Bernal Diaz was born. His first hand account of the conquest of Mexico, begun in his seventies, is amazingly detailed through an old soldiers eyes. Motivated by the inaccuracies of other chroniclers, his pursuit was to set the record straight(BD p.7). If he had not survived, we might not have had his insight, and if Rustichello had not been a fellow prisoner, the discovery of the New World may well have been delayed.

By the time Bernal Diaz and Cortes entered Mexico, Spain was considered the defender of the true faith. Proselytizing Christianity became a holy mission, a dual purpose alongside the quest for gold, highlighted when confronted with the barbarity of sacrifices and cannibalism(BD p.37) which is practiced throughout the entire region. Like Polo, Cortes considers them idolators and urges Montezuma to embrace the true faith and reject sacrifices and his devilish idols(BD p.125). Military campaigns, one of ruthless hordes and the other a skilled few, demonstrate brilliant tactics and state of the art warfare determining the course of two continents and influencing the entire world. Cortes, with only a handful of men, but armed with muskets, crossbows, and horses(BD p.76), was able to subjugate an entire peoples. The Mongols, each with 20 horses, had unheard of speed, a tactical advantage where they would divide and attack. They had excellent fighting skills, a precise chain of command, and were the first to use smoke screens. They never lost a battle.

Both invaders had determined, fierce, yet benevolent leaders. Kubilai Khan, described as an average man(MP p.122), was able to command a vast empire with undying loyalty. Cortes, pictured by many as a ruthless conquerer, shows compassion when he is reluctant to kill(BD p.70), justice when he arrests Montezumas tax collectors(BD p.111), and wisdom when he forces two tribes to make peace(BD p.120). Both leaders demonstrate magnetic personalities, vision, and transcendent wisdom

Fortuitous events are present for each author. If the priests had not refused to accompany Marco's father and uncle on their second trip, he may not have been able to go, and spend the next twenty years in the Khan's service. And in that time, travelling across the world was a perilous and dangerous journey. Coming under the Khan's favor and able with his blesssing to traverse numerous kingdoms with alacrity was especially fortunate.

Cortes seems favored beyond description. Escaping with the fleet before being recalled by a fearful and vacillating Governor Velazquez, defeating what became his most valuable allies, the Tlascalans(BD p.164), and recieving his most precious asset in the form of his interpreter, Dona Marina, enabled him to confront and subdue an entire nation with a pitiful few.

Common threads and themes consist throughout both novels. Religion, as a driving force, pervades and rationalizes each author in their travels. Powerful, wilful visionaries who can move nations. Tremendous battles with historic implications. Greed and the need for wealth and power. Political maneuverings using guile, wit, and uncanny perception. All the ingredients for oscar winning movies that are the real history of mankind

Recorded history is rampant with magnificent figures that transcend the average man and steer civilization in their own way. Duplicitous actions by enemies, treason, and subterfuge provide the backdrop for the heroic and victorious.

Marco Polo and Cortes are two of the foundations for the "Age of Discovery". Though initially motivated by the siren call of gold. They must surely have known their places in history and of the magnificent times in which they were living. All these early wanderers seem to share more than personal ambition. Curiosity

Work Cited

Polo, Marco. <u>The Travels</u>. Trans. Ronald Latham. England: Penguin, 1958.

Diaz, Bernal. <u>The Conquest of New Spain</u>. Trans. J.M. Cohen.
England: Penguin, 1963.

***

" GODDAMITT, WHAT DO YOU MEAN THE SHITTER
WON'T FLUSH?"

Mulroy was livid. Waving his dirty hands, stretching his
chins into the head yet refusing to step into the space where I and
another stood in two inches of murky water. " I wanna catch this
fucker."

It wasn't a new thing. From time to time, throughout the ship,
someone was stuffing rolls of toilet paper into the bowls knowing
the results. I hid a grin as Mulroy, face red, body and chins shaking,
turned to the phone. After a few moments Mulroy returned," Stay
where you are, don't trek that shit into the compartment, The Turd
Chasers will be here shortly."

The Turd Chasers. Actually HT's, or Hull Technicians, who
were in charge of the piping system on the ship. Not their primary
purpose, being qualified welders and metalworkers, but they were
the ship's plumbers and the ones to call for these emergencies.
And don't call them Turd Chasers.

A huge figure filled the doorway. I turned to see a man in
blue coveralls, red haired chest exposed, first class chevrons on
lapels, with a blonde haired, red cheeked youth peering over his
shoulder. " Which one is it?" He said. My companion replied,"
Outboard." He turned to the youth and ordered," Hook the hose
where I showed you and bring the other end in here." The youth
nodded and disappeared.

" We'll have to suck all three," He said, " Hook up inboard."
The youth, as new as I was, stepped into the flooded space with
determination. Red observed as his "Boot", short for Boot Camp,
did as told. " Now I need you to stick your head into that shitter
and let me know when it bubbles, we don't wanna oversuck."

With conscientious observation the youth bent to the shitter. Red disappeared. Echoing from above Red's voice said," IS HE WATCHING?" My companion said," YEAH!"

Suddenly all three shittters exploded from one hundred and twenty five pounds per square inch of ships fire main. Shocked and stunned by the explosion I saw the youth turn towards us, eyes clamped shut, face dotted with white and brown specks, digging toilet paper from his lips. Blinded, clearing his eyes with one hand and fingers digging deeply scraping shit from his mouth I heard a muted wail. Mulroy and Red appeared in the doorway laughing. I couldn't help but giggle cleaning the white stuff, brown stuff, and puke for the rest of the morning. Tough job for tough men. Hoorah.

***

1970

Reno, Nevada. An Adult Disneyland just like Las Vegas only smaller and in the northern part of the state. Winter had settled in by the time I got there. A cold gust made me shiver as I got off the bus. I walked into the terminal and there he was. My father, dressed in suit and tie and a broad grin. He hugged me. We were about eye level and I could see the genes. An older me yet different.

When your sixteen year old son shows up on your doorstep, bearing another man's name, or two, a man must have some reservations. The sense of propriety must be mitigated by the sense of loss. He never hit me, nor even more than show disappointment in my behavior at times. I was still a good kid, and after he toured me downtown, the lights and environment glazing my mind, I made it clear I had three immediate goals. To get my drivers license, and car, and to graduate from high school.

Dad had a unit in a trailer park in Sparks. Next to a drive-in theatre. He was working the swing shift downtown at the Cal-Neva so that most nights I was on my own. The first week we shopped for some clothes, drove his dune buggy, and got me registered in high school.

It was the opening year for this high school, Reno was growing, and because of that it was only serving 10th and 11th grades with the 12th the next year. As a Junior I would be in the first graduating class. It only took 30 minutes to walk. I was set. Now all I needed was a job.

A couple of weeks passed, school now a routine, when Dad mentioned that a hotel casino had openings it its coffee shop for busboys. He drove me downtown, we went in and I filled out an application with the Hostess. I was hired. I started that week with a couple of swing shifts during the week, the Hostess allowing for bus rides from Sparks after school, and on the day shift on weekends. Besides the nepotism of the Cab Co., it was my first real job, a busboy at the Mapes Hotel Casino.

***

Organismic Analogy

If humanity can shape God after its own image, it is not so far fetched to portray society in the same light. Each aspect equal to or functioning as though it were a part of a human body. After the French Revolution, many thinkers began to do so. Joseph de Maistre, a minister for nobility, considered a 'body politic' with a head, arms, body and legs for nobles, warriors, and peasants. He believed in soveriegn law, wherein the people, considered stupid, must live in traditional institutions, under the leadership of kings. Count Henri de St. Simon felt that society must operate on moral consensus, that individuals have no rights, but duties. He thought religion as essential to social control and that the basic unit was the family, not the individual. Then there was Auguste Comte, a student of St. Simon, who thought of society as an organism, when all parts are working, in harmony and balance, that the state was the organism and that social forces worked through the institutions/

117

tissues. He felt that biological organisms are immutable but that social organisms were capable of improvement. Development of the group mind equaled progress

Stating that evolution drives the universe, Herbert Spencer noted that many species formed societies such as bees, ants, and birds, and that societies evolved according to physical laws. Human societies, with their complexity, would be termed the Super Organic. Each society would be a form of struggle for existence and when all the forces are in balance, equilibration. Conflict was endemic. Militarism rose from the surplus agriculural production which in turn led to Industrialism and Laissez-Faire economics. Though a contemporary of Marx, he said that if you leave the market alone, humans will become better humans

These nineteenth century analogies were continued by the likes of Evans-Pritchard in his studies of the Nuer, age groups as being cohesive elements, and Mary Douglas, his student who, like Spencer, in symbolism only, compared the human body as symbols for society.(Mcgee, 470

Its logical to compare aspects of society to symbols of the human body. The thought synthesizes complexities of civilization into normal biological workings. Easier for the mind of man, in psychological terms, to grasp the world around him

***

Spring, 1971

As a minor I wasn't supposed to go into the Casino, my job specifically relating to the Coffee shop. But there were times when providing the cocktail waitresses with coffee, condiments, or other errands, I could spend some moments watching the activities.

I knew from Dad how it worked, he being a Pit Boss. There were the slot machines, commonly referred to as the One Armed Bandits, spread peripherially around the main event, The Tables. The Tables constituted groups of green clothed, six seated arena's where good looking men and women dealt blackjack or other table games that were popular. Each was grouped in circles, each a Pit. Of course the Craps Tables were the epicenter of action located specifically in front of the main entrance opposite the Roulette Wheels. Then there was Keno, a numbers game extracted from Asia, from one to eighty, occupied one corner with seating. Keno runners in short skirts and high heels toured the casino for players, waitresses plied the Bandits and Tables for drinks and tips. So long as one was gambling, drinks were free. And in another corner by the bar was the stage for the nightly bands, several tables in front, open to the general public.

But my job was in the coffee shop. I cleaned tables, resetting places, making coffee in the huge urns, refilling cups, providing icewater, resupplying napkins, straws, ice, and generally running errands for the girls. I took special glee in meeting the customers with a coffee pot in hand. The girls had light yellow dresses which invariably got smudged, us boys wore gold smocks. All of us wore nametags. The Hostess, with nametag, always dressed in tasteful attire, escorted customers to their seats. Always apportioning fairness in order give all the girls their fair share.

Tips, the lifeblood of a gambling town. Bartenders, Barbacks, Dealers, Keno Runners, Coctail Waitresses, and Bus Boys all depended on them. After shifts many would go to other casino's and spread the wealth. Once, a Dealer who had befriended me, having a cup of coffee at the counter, left a big tip. As he got up to go he said," Ya know, we have a saying around here. Keeps everyone going when the times are tough. It works too. 'What comes around goes around.' Always leave a good tip, ya hear."

What comes around goes around.

The girls liked me and the tips were good, tips coming as a percentage of the girls take. Since I had no bills, with Dad's assistance practicing with the Dune Buggy, I managed to save my paychecks plus and in 3 months got my license and bought a 64' baby blue Volkswagon with sunroof. A proud moment.

Driving to school, as well as work, was special. I was a part of humanity, equal to my peers. Despite the obstacles, I had achieved. Peer pressure was certainly part of it, but an inner longing, an instinctual desire, demanded that I become a part of life. The Big Picture. In entering this Big Picture, was it cultural grooming or instinct that had dictated my actions. Defiance?

***

Mutable. 1.liable or subject to change.2. given to changing or constantly changing (The Random House Dictionary, concise edition, ninth printing, 1988)

Within the dimensions of human understanding, it should be acknowledged that we are a mutable species. This mutability can be appreciated both culturally and biologically as we resurrect ourselves from a deliquescent past through written history, theory, conjecture, and a rising cache of anthopological artifacts. Recent history alone serves notice as to the mutability of culture. But the cornerstone of all change, and the central basis for anthropology, is evolution. Evolution, the forces of which, unknown until Mendel, enabled a rodent like primate to become a bipedal, cerebral creature with the ability to adapt to any environment. And as these superior organisms learned to master their surroundings it became necessary to teach and nurture their young. Identifying their niche, cataloguing the world around them, and passing this information from generation to generation became the fabric of all societies and the glue of culture, Language. This was first expressed in Europe in 1750 by Anne Robert Jacques Turgot:

Possessor of a treasure of signs which he has the faculty of multiplying to infinity, he (man) is able to assure the retention of his acquired ideas, to communicate them to other men, and to transmit them to his successors as a constantly expanding heritage. (Langness,1)

Whether the path we took began with the Visual Predation Theory or the Arboreal Theory, or whether it was a continuous trip like Phyletic Gradualism or a leapfrogging Punctuated Equilibrium, we are indeed a masterful product of nature, whose ability to nurture, created a species whose conscious thought and inexhaustible desire for more knowledge is most manifest within the last 100 years. In the words of Pico Mirandola 15th century, regarding human dignity,"We are the eyes of the Universe."

If, in fact, anatomically modern humans have remained the same for the last 200,000 years, it could be assumed that our ancestors had the same propensity for thought and discovery as we do today. And it is their foundations upon which early civilizations stood. The Sumerians, Egyptians, Babylonians, and Pre-Socratics paved the way for the Greeks and ultimately Western civilization. And within, as well as between, cultures changed from diffusion and philosophies. How they viewed themselves within the order of things is a question that has been handed down through the ages. Nature or Nurture?

Unlike Hegel, I would not don seven league boots and bypass the 6th and 17th centuries until I saw Descartes and,"Cry land like a sailor." Though not wrong in assuming this a time of intellectual despair, it was also a time in which the means to pursue that question of nature vs. nurture could be resumed. The transition from feudalism, the establishment of universities, canon law, and the acclimatization of the newly found works of Aristotle initiated renewed inquiries into the nature of man. Boethius' injunction to "join faith with reason" was replaced with a new dualism placing reason alongside faith

"Cogito Ergo Sum" was Descartes' proof that there is a God. But it was also his position that each of us is born with innate ideas that can be infinitely expanded, and that these ideas are the source of true knowledge. And, as in Plato's day, a thesis is met with an antithesis. "To be is to be percieved" was Berkely's response. A colleague of John Locke who declared that the mind is *Tabula Rasa* at birth, a blank slate upon which all knowledge is experiential, through the senses. Now it was "Psychic Unity" vs. Innate

In answer to humankinds quest, most manifest within the last 100 years, to seek more knowledge, and our place in the universe, comes a new science, Anthropology. And, in recognizing our mutability, it is the science of human cultural and biological variation and evolution. From Australopithecines to neanderthals, Mayans to couch potato's, it embraces an holistic approach in measuring the context and scope of human existence on this planet. Is it Nature or is it Nurture which has most fundamentally affected our growth and development? Or could it be a blend of both? Could not the nurturing of culture be a template over the natural world? But if hunting, or scavenging, is 9/10's of our existence, isn't it still only one aspect of culture? These are questions that, if not necessarily answered, are given broader perspective within this new science

The debate between Descartes and Locke applies. We know that we inherit physical characteristics from our parents, might we not also acquire certain traits, predispositions, and emotional makeup as well? When Descartes presupposes innate ideas, where did he get that idea from? And if we are *Tabula Rasa* at birth, why does a child instinctively suckle? I would contend that through observation, and an inherited intellectual capacity, they were, like all of us, attempting to place order in the universe. They had not, within their own cultural framework, the concept of evolution, nor the early influence of a charismatic grandfather.

Imperious man, who rules the bestial crowd,
Of Language, reason, and reflection proud,
With brow erect, who scorns this earthly sod,
And styles himself the image of his God;
Arose from rudiments of form and sense,
An embryon point, or microscopic ens!

from *The Temple of Nature*
by
Erasmus Darwin

***

Summer, 1971

Talking to Mom, at least once a week, it was decided that I would return to Maryland for the summer. After all, I was her baby and I missed her. I flew back for about 6 weeks and settled in. Hanging out at the pool, fooling around with the guys, spending time with Mom.

In my absence they had hired another guy to work at the station. And it wasn't the same station either, having moved to another location. No gas pumps. It seemed the company was slowly slipping. At least they still had a mechanic for the cabs. I stood outside waiting and watching the mechanic, while his helper, my replacement, silently kept to himself in the corner. I wondered how they kept him busy.

They were having a meeting in the front office. Larry pulled up in one of the company cabs looking jittery. He walked straight up to the front office not saying anything. After a few minutes the mechanic rose from the hood, closed it, and said," I'm taking this baby out for a spin." The helper nodded. The mech revved it up, pulled out of the bay, and turned right down the street.

Screaming erupted from the front. Sounds like a body being slammed against the wall. The door flew open and Larry darted out, shirt ripped, and started running through the bay. Ted was right behind him booming," I WANT MY FUKIN MONEY YOU FUK."

But Larry was faster, spurred by fear, briefly stumbling he quickly recovered and dashed out. Except for the shock of it, it would have been comical the way he ran full bore down the street with only one shoe on one foot, sock flapping from the other. Ted turned back to the office and closed the door. I looked down and there was one colorful suede shoe. I never saw Larry again.

A couple days before departure back to Reno I called Dad to confirm flight and arrival times. He seemed hesitant to talk. I said, "Is something wrong?". He said, "No, ah...ah... when you get home I gotta surprise for you." I said," Yeah? What is it?" He said," ah... I'll tell ya when ya get here." It seemed that he didn't expect me back.

Well, it was a surprise allright, but I guess it was a fair trade. Seems that Dad took to driving my car in my absence instead of his light blue Cadillac. He never fully explained to me what happened but the fact was that my car was totaled, or just plain gone. In return I got to scoot around town in the green Dune Buggy. It didn't matter the Bug had no heater. Even in the dead of winter I would be cool.

***

Fall, 1971

I wasn't going to argue. Transcripts and testings had allowed me extra credits. For my entire Senior year I only needed to go to class half days. I spent the extra time reading fantasies like 'Lord of the Rings' and science fiction in the form of the Foundation series by Isaac Asimov. Of course, I added hours at the Coffee Shop too.

Whenever possible I and some friends would tour the city. We explored all the neighborhoods and, at night, we would parade, like every other teen in town, and especially on Friday and Saturday nights, the main drag, Virginia Street. Virginia Street sliced, north and south, down the middle of the casino's. Approaching from the north, past the University, across the I-80 bridge, and passing under the arch that read," The Biggest Little City in the World.", we would honk horns and wave at each other in youthful release. The glittering lights and tourists were fascinating. Here, with visitors from every corner and walk of life, was a crossroads of humanity.

Of course, the underlying principle and reason for existence of such a town was gambling, the quick buck, greed. But in contrast to that, though many were transients, the full time residents lived as morally and upstanding as anywhere else. Just making a living, raising families, looking to the future.

He was a big shot the first night. He had been lavish with tips, buying friends, even treating the band to drinks and they in turn bantering with him while onstage. The whole casino seemed to admire him. The bar, short a barback, needed some ice and I volunteered. I passed behind him with a bucket of ice. He was wearing a bright red suit, white satin shirt with red tie and red shoes. He had just gotten up from his seat at the blackjack table, drink in hand, approaching the band pointing a finger at the lead singer. "Hey, I like your shirts, you guys wear the same underwear?" The band laughed. The Dealer, chuckling, motioned him back to his seat. A cocktail waitress came by and he directed her to give the band a round and tipped her. The Dealer smiled attractively as he placed a bet for her. He was where the action was at.

The second night he was a loser. Still short a barback, it was now my job to bring the ice. There he was, sitting at the corner of the bar, same suit, wrinkled, right shirt flap out, and tie loosened with the knot dangling awkwardly. When the band arrived and took the stage he rose with drink in hand and waved at them. The lead singer said," Haven't I seen that suit before?" Dismissed, he turned towards the dealers. They ignored him. Suddenly he screamed." I LOST TWELVE THOUSAND DOLLARS IN HERE LAST NIGHT, DO I GET ANY RESPECT ?" Silence. He turned to the Pit boss who had kissed his ass the night before. "WHAT? I CAN'T GET ANOTHER DRINK?", wobbling and swaying from his binge. Then he turned to the pretty Dealer whom he'd tipped heavily the night before that was avoiding him. " HEY BITCH, DON'T YOU REMEMBER ME?" Security, who had been watching for hours, quickly descended and escorted his broke ass out. Another victim, a GEORGE, he paid the house, paid the people, now get the fuck outta here.

***

A flaming asshole. I've seen one, really. It was in my first year in military school. Hanging out at my fraternity I would gaze expectantly towards senior cadets for guidance and knowledge. The smallest steps towards manhood the largest.

I'd spend time in the Key House watching my fraternity brothers. As most guys think farts are funny and as most young men are prone to experiment it had become not unusual to see one of my mentors suddenly jump to the center, lie flat on his back, knees to his elbows, legs spread wide, and light a flame to his ass. Laughter erupted as a blue green flame, accompanied by the appropriate sound, disturbed our studies.

Big Brothers are teachers. Once accepted they tend to be open, inhibitions removed, and display youthful courage in accepted arena's. One was a well respected significant member of the Lacross team, 11th grade and hairy as hell. The baked beans had been good to us. Jocular and competitive the guys jumped to the center, legs spread, and demonstrated their manhood. Us newbies laughed like hell .

Lacross, a kind and compassionate buckaroo, decided to up the stakes. Spontaneously reacting to the last performer he snagged the lighter, pulled his military green pants and underwear down, and took position. Covering his hardware with one hand we saw the other hand place a flame dangerously close to one hairy ass. He must have saved it for a while. Eyes squinting for a big one we saw him grunt and a spectacular bloom, sound muffled, erupted. It was a big one. I saw his eyes grow wide as the flame first singed the hairs surrounding and quickly entered his anus. We escorted him to the infirmary. Two days later he came back to less than heroic acclamations. Personally speaking, farting in public could be painful.

***

Marlowe and Swift: On Human Nature

The evolution of human thought, how mankind views mankind, what our primal and innate characteristics and dispositions contain and how God does and does not figure in our destinies, is chronicled in our written histories. Empiricism, Rationalism, and Skepticism are schools of thought born of the cultural and political conditions of the times. Since man emerged from a tribal existence, an egalitarian society, to nation states, where class distinctions with disparate realities are clearly defined, there have been those who would explore our inner selves. Insights are gained, and we can vicariously travel back in time and sense through these authors their concepts and views on human nature. Christopher Marlowe (1564-1593), and Johnathan Swift (1667-1745), products of the Renaissance both question tradition and authority, and display our nature to destroy ourselves. Marlowe, whose <u>Dr. Faustus</u> is a figure of personal tragedy, and Swift, whose juvenalian satire laments the systematic oppression of the Irish, shows the pallette of human nature in its quest for knowledge, power, curiosity, hubris, and ambition. Both, I believe, Swift admits it, are misanthropists.

The Renaissance attitudes in Marlowe's play are influenced by medieval thought. The central character is a renowned Doctor who seeks the necromantic power offered by the dark prince. Initially, the newfound power he desires will be applied to good works, but of course the frail nature of man is dominant:

How am I glutted with conceit of this!
Shall I make spirits fetch me what I please?
Resolve me of all ambiguities?
Perform what desperate enterprise I will?

Faustus, for this power, signs his soul off to the devil despite warnings. But instead of the envisioned good works, he wastes his power and ultimately is called to hell. And in the end, he truly realizes what he has done.

Though Dr.Faustus may actually be based on a real person of some disrepute, I believe that many of the attitudes displayed are shared by the author. Cerebral and eloquent, his characters reflect the darker side of human nature. Marlowe seems to have religious beliefs but questions the institutions and foundations of medieval thought. He challenges the system. He shows that human nature is flawed. Man cannot be Godlike, he is subject to greed, lust, and capricious behavior. Unable to save himself from his own destruction. Questions emerge, and in those questions shows his own philosophy on human nature. Is Faustus noble, in the beginning or in the end when he repents? Is curiosity a vice or a virtue? Ambition? Power? Wealth? And in the end is it man's nature to be weak willed, one step away from being anathema to God? It seems so.

***

December 31, 1971

New Years Eve. I and a fellow busboy were dedicated to assist in the festivities, special to be sure, in the SkyRoom, top floor of the hotel. One of the best places in town to be to bring in the new year. High dollar people paid high dollars to be there. Prior to the suits and gowns arriving, we and others spent furious efforts setting tables, glasses and silverware spotless, and staging the salads and appetizers for the well to do. Once finished we waited, breathless, for our customers to arrive.

He was a questionable fellow, long haired and somewhat devious, but we were paired in stead of the ex con and the middle aged, obvious pervert, unacceptable, who were my counterparts in the Coffee Shop. I liked the guy, unlike the others, only a couple of years older, who kept me chuckling with his behind the kitchen descriptions of the fat, ugly, and deviant customers.

By the time we'd hauled all the prime rib and lobsters from the service elevator the party had started. The girls frantically serving drinks and meals to those accustomed to servility. The band had started and soon high dollar suits and gowns were hopping to the featured act. As spaces cleared we were supposed to remove plates and bowls. Soon my partner discovered that the complimentary bottles of champagne, no bigger than a beer bottle, could be removed by us and replaced on request. We took advantage. By the time the new year rang in we, in the alcove by the service elevator, guzzled more champagne, ate more prime rib and buttered lobster, than anyone else on the floor. Drunk with this funny sumbitch, I giggled at the thought that this was the year I was graduating from high school.

***

Mom was determined to have me back. Dad had no argument to keep me. She offered me a car and tuition to the local community college. I was still an emotional game of tag.

But it was really no contest, I was still the Momma's boy. I agreed to fly back. And really, I think Dad was willing to see me go. I was the child he'd never planned for. The child that would have best never have happened. Affections best shared from a distance. He'd never recovered from being adopted himself and once informed decided, with stubborn ignorance, not to finish the fifth grade. It seemed that every time he looked at me he saw my mother, and every time I looked at him I saw a me I didn't like. He'd always made the motions, said the right things, but I could tell. (ah...ah... I gotta surprise for ya.).

Graduation wasn't a big thing, just a formal affair I didn't need. The night before my fellow students walked the aisle, shook hands, and posed for family, I was on a plane back to Maryland. I recieved my diploma in the mail.

***

Summer, 1972

Herman had found a good deal with a used car salesman. It was an ancient white Comet. In less than a week it broke down with a bad rear seal. Unrepairable. Mom hit the roof. We went car shopping and, through a friend, purchased a light green Monte Carlo only 2 years old. Cool.

I needed some income. I managed to secure a job at the local mall selling shoes. I needed to be established before I attended college in the fall. That's where I met Toes.

Toes was a Viet Nam Veteran, with wife and child, proud of his ancestry, listing ancestors with military service. Exploits in the field had provided him with a different aspect to life. Almost sacreligious. He was a good man, we bonded. Whenever we met in the back searching for a customers size he'd describe the anomalies of his targets feet. Fat toes, skinnny toes, flippers, I was pressed to keep composure when I stepped out and analyzed his assessments.

One day I came in on the afternoon shift and saw a huge middle aged white woman, fat bulging out of a dress two sizes too small, with seven boxes and shoes splayed in disarray around the most enormous feet I'd ever seen. I entered the back to hang up my jacket and there was Toes.

I said," What's up?"

" Did you see Gigantor out there?" Rolling his eyes and shaking his head. " Bitch insists she wears two sizes less than GI-FUKIN-GANTIC!" He was depressed, I could tell. "Shit man, I had three of those toes with my eggs this morning. I don't think I can do this shit anymore, I gotta kid to feed and this fukin place ain't doing it!" His shoulders slumped, a look of despair in his eyes," I gotta chance for this job, a stable future for my family but I need a high school diploma or at least a GED." I said," Hell Man, you can do it, if I could I'd do it for ya." He said," Yeah?"

It was a plan. He was scared to take the test and fail. It would have been a dead end for him, devastating. I'd have done it for nothing but he insisted on paying me fifty bucks. Registering for the next GED testings, and placing my picture instead of his on the pass, coordinating our days off, he drove me to Baltimore for the required exams. As Mr. Big Toes I applied myself, along with others striving to accomplish, for my friend. We passed and he got the job.

***

Race and Intelligence

What is IQ? Is it quantifiable? Can a number indicate one person's ability of cognitive thought? If not for intelligence, humankind would not be communicating on the Internet, orbiting the earth, or have the means of discovering their own origins. But assigning an IQ to a particular person or race has been used to support ideological and racial superiority rather than identifying one's deficiencies. Do Intelligence tests measure intelligence or cultural adeptness, is it inherited or not? Are we entering a period of stratification and class structure based on cognitive abilities? What is Intelligence?

Controversial? You bet. The Frenchman Binet had no clue to what he was unleashing when he administered his test to poor students in order to identify learning deficiencies. Others, like Goddard, would utilize such means to classify immigrants and support his position of segregation against violating the purity of a superior race. Such acts have been and should be denounced as inherently wrong. But the concept persists, and reached high volume when "The Bell Curve" was published

"The Bell Curve" used statistics of general intelligence testing to indicate many of the reasons of social ills. Using figures derived from the white population, class distinction, poverty, welfare, crime, unemployment, and affirmative action were addressed with supposed objectivity and dealt a severe blow to the concept of equality as we know it.

In refutation, Stephen J. Gould, published "The Mismeasure of Man". In it he disputed hereditary intelligence as a fallacy and renewed the faith in acknowledging all humankind with equal ability towards growth and development, equal cognitive abilities, equal ability to rise within society held back only by motivation, industry, and effort. I have personal reflections which seem to indicate the extreme measures and illogicality of pigeon holing people according to a bad test day, or the extreme efforts to "level the playing field" regardless of cognitive ability but merely to create a demographic picture of ultimate fairness.

I myself come from the lower socio-economic spectrum. A first generation college student, not to mention retired sailor, I know that ability is an ephemeral element that is only displayed with effort. Different people have different abilities. An education is nice but it does not give a true reflection of cognitive ability. The ability to learn, if one is given the proper motivation and incentive has been proven to me available to all races regardless of background and economic status. Only cultural taboos based on racial distinctions hold individuals back.

When I joined the Navy, the instrument for assigning personnel according to their abilities was called the GCT/ARI (General Comprehension Test and Arithmetic). It has since been called the ASVAB and now the AFQT. Though touted as a tool to indicate ability to perform tasks and numerically it appears to be relatively successful in apportioning qualified individuals to their careers, it is not infallible. I have worked with individuals of less "cognitve" rates whose superior performance clearly showed anomalies in the system. I have also operated with those whom tout some intangible evidence of mental superiority and were dumber than a box of hair.

On the other hand I have also sat on boards where social engineering was administered regardless of performance or ability. The word "demographics" still leaves a sour taste in my mouth for the way it was used to promote personnel and provide the unqualified opportunities they didn't deserve. This only to provide a demographic picture of "equal opportunity" where in fact it was reverse discrimination. There are no clear answers to our social problems. The pendulum seems to swing at high octane to either side. I expect a lively debate in class.

***

Summer, 1972

One of the guys was having a party. It was a chance to meet girls. I was still a virgin and believed in true love. Wanted it, felt it was natural. I was terribly horny. When most my age had known intimacy there was still a vast unknown in my mind. I was desperate for a girl friend, a trust, a partner. Still I was choosy, or scared of giving myself indiscriminately. Bold with the guys, shy with the ladies, whenever both were in the room I was a wall flower. Dancer still a memory.

Despite those times in diapers, and desperate pleas to Mom for privacy in both bedroom and bath, I had never shown myself to another woman except once. It wasn't a good thing.

It started as a lark. Fooling around, in macho style, with my high school friends. We decided to drive, east on I-80, out of Reno, to the infamous, or famous, Mustang Ranch. I parked my Volkswagon in the lot. We piled out and approached the fence. A sign by the gate said,' Ring the Buzzer.' We did. In return we heard a hum at the gate and pulled it open. We walked the walk to the front door of what seemed a connecting series of mobile homes. We entered.

Approaching the center of the lobby there was a flurry of ladies, in bikini's and high heels, lining up for inspection. Suddenly I didn't want to be there. The process seemed too impersonal, too cavalier. Once lined up each girl gave her name, certainly not the real one, and smiled in a provocative manner, or lewd. All we had to do was pick one. Each was several years older than any of us. They seemed to share a secret, noting our youth, giggling and sharing looks while we stared. My buddies made their selections and disappeared.

I stood there alone. Burdened, and stressed, by the knowing greedy looks, I quickly pointed towards a lady my size. I think she said 'Trixie'. She scanned the other ladies with a confident smile and led me away. The room seemed to have mirrors everywhere. Initiating small talk to alleviate my nervousness, she motioned me to the bed and began undressing me.

She tried. But some force inside refused my body to obey. I couldn't perform. It was as if I were watching from afar. Some force inside was blocking a natural instinct. Gratefully, after strenuous activity on her part, she gave up claiming my time was up. What? these things were timed? I gratefully got dressed while she removed herself to the bathroom to 'freshen up'. We walked back together to the lobby where my friends were waiting. Trixie sat down with a friend and whispered in her ear. As we left I noticed Trixie and her friend staring at me with a look of pity in their eyes. I was quiet on the drive back. I still hadn't realized manhood.

The party was in full swing by the time I arrived. I joked with the guys, compatriots in The Woods, and soon found myself sitting in the corner, watching. Two sisters were sitting on the couch, one joking, the other, the older sister, quietly observing, gazed in my direction. Our eyes met. Some connection, or spark of hidden knowledge passed between us. Still too shy to make the first move, she managed to extricate herself from her litttle sister and sat beside me. Two young minds meeting, sharing philosophies and beliefs. I had found a counterpart, a female mind filled with intelligence and thought, not to mention a tall, quiet, and regal presence. She was only one year younger but I sensed the quality of her soul and the purity of her mind. Sunshine.

She gave me her name and phone number. She had beautiful handwriting. Calligraphy compared to my script. Like a form of art, an expression of the mind for the world to see.

***

Summary

With the exception of the caves of Lascaux, I've had little exposure to rock art and its intriguing meanings, much less its ubiquitous nature right here in Nevada. It is disconcerting that without reliable dating we cannot determine a chronology and thereby assign definitions or meanings from which we can determine thought processes and their evolutions, cosmologies, and compare with ethnographies. Until a breakthrough in technology, or a North American "Rosetta Stone" emerges to unveil the mysteries of these pre-historic peoples we can only theorize and conjecture about their world view and lifestyles. But we have some things we can work with. That human physiology has not changed much since then, nor todays mind as we know it (the workings of the nervous system is a good baseline), the regional environment is relatively the same (since 11000 bp), and the urge for procreation is as universal as the need for subsistence.

We can also draw on present phenomena other than extant indigenous peoples. Urban gangs, though under different societal pressures, through their graffiti, express territoriality, warnings, and beliefs. Even the frustrated adolescent who leaves his name on the water tower is acting in tandem with the lovers who carve their names in a tree. Each group or individual visually displaying an intangible commonality with preliterate peoples, the need to put their mark on the world, be heard, and understood. Rock Art is the marks from the past, we have heard, it is our duty to understand, not only for them but for ouselves as well.

***

You'd never know they were cousins, Fancy and Cherrie. Fancy always wearing work clothes that consisted of flannel shirts, bluejeans, and boots underlining a handsome but plain face and short brown hair parted in the middle while Cherrie invariably wore the latest fashions highlighting a slim attractive frame and coal black hair brushed back to reveal a pixie face. Where Cherrie always flirted with the guys, Fancy was taciturn. Though both were the same size and shared at least some features, two more dissimilar individuals would never be thought related.

It seemed like old times riding in the car. The girls up front, Fancy driving, and us guys in back with the pool sticks. Sitting behind Fancy, driving, I had a good look at Cherrie. She still talked as if the world revolved around her, Fancy nodding to the soliloquy. But from my seat I could see her wings and sensed loss. Unlike Fancy whose wings were broad, colorful, and untroubled, Cherrie's looked wilted, stunted, with a sad gray dominating. Maybe it wasn't like old times after all.

We filed into Smitty's in single file nodding to the cheers of the regulars for our first match of the season. The crowd was all there. A mixture of differing economic lives. From Lawyers, retired cops, construction workers, guys and gals, this place drew from all aspects of humanity. Because in this neighborhood, Smitty's, due to it's place and time, attracted the memories of more than one generation.

The cheers silenced as we took our reserved perch by the dance floor overlooking the pool table. As we took our seats beneath the ' NADS ' sign our fans began chanting..... GO-NADS, GO-NADS, GO-NADS ... until we waved them off. The challenging team, from another bar, was already there practicing.

They were the Conquistadores. They were one of our major rivals when we last played. I remembered a rough bar filled with fishermen and inhospitable to strangers. Their style was tough, wooden, but very effective. We were evenly matched.

After nods and greetings Sugar and Garr had exchanged paperwork and we were ready to play. Cherrie was up first and so was The Turk. They flipped coins, Cherrie called," Tails", and it turned up heads. Turk's break.

Cherrie's wings were blinking a timid yellow and pink as she racked, turned, and returned to her seat. Turk circled the table like a bear circling a wounded seal pup. As his wings came into view my heart hardened. His were a vultures wings, blood red and dark brown. The life he saw had become a limited view.

The large balding black bearded man broke the balls with thunderous force. Making two stripes on the break, he proceeded to make four more with mechanical precision leaving one near the pocket and the eight ball in the middle of the table.

Turk glared at Cherrie as she rose to grab her stick. He turned to the grunts of his fellow players grinning while Cherrie assessed the table. She made two balls and bounced another against the bank leaving Turk a straight -in shot. He made it and left the cue ball directly behind the eight in the side. He said," Side Pocket", and stroked it with condescending force.

Cherrie turned towards her seat shaking her head at us in apology. Sugar smiled and gave a thumbs up as I said," It's a long season." Fancy rose saying," Gimme dat stick." Cherrie handed it over and walked to the juke box. Her eyes rose and there was Dexter, her high school sweetheart. Now working for his Dad at the gas station we hadn't seen much of him lately. As Cherrie closed the distance with Dexter her wings seemed to brighten with a bluish green before they disappeared.

***

Time does not heal all wounds. And for those who say they wouldn't change a thing, if given the chance to do it all over again, are either liars or content with an outcome they wouldn't jeopardize by changing the past.

I've done it again. It used to take years, now only months. During my travels it had always been a priority to find a neighborhood bar I could call my own. Blend in with the locals, share jokes and philosophies, and play pool with the best of them. But the cycle, process, or syndrome has increased in speed with age. Drinking to excess, dancing by myself, and challenging others with a false manhood and arrogance has ostracized me from every watering hole I've claimed. Romancing the ladies, then, once conquered, dropping them like dishrags. This isn't the me I remember. This isn't the moral, caring, fun to be with kind of guy I remember nor the way I want to be remembered.

I know the problem. The invisible cross I carry, unbelievably heavy, weighing down my heart and soul, preventing me from the courage to succeed in anything. A burden that only becomes less mindful through the debilitating effects of alcohol. It is a guilt. A guilt born in the opening chapter of my adult life. A time when young men emerge from childhood with dreams and convictions, ready to tackle the world with optimism and confidence. But for me a confidence crushed, optimism negated, convictions questioned, dreams erased. What is a life lived in regret compared to death with honor? Is there no greater pain than to have one's heart ripped out at the threshold of manhood?

If I could change the past I would. If I could reach back in time......

***

" This fall I think you're riding for - it's a special kind of fall, a horrible kind. The man falling isn't permitted to feel or hear himself hit bottom. He just keeps falling and falling. The whole arrangement's designed for men who, at some time or other in their lives, were looking for something their own environment couldn't supply them with. Or they thought their own environment couldn't supply them with. So they gave up looking. They gave it up before they really even got started. You follow me?"

Mr. Antolini to Holden Caulfield in 'The Catcher in the Rye"

***

December, 1972

Tap Tap Tap Tap Tap Tap Tap Tap.........Tap Tap Tap Tap Tap......Tap Tap Tap Tap Tap

"GODDAMIT YOU KNOW I'M BUSY, HOLD YOUR HORSES", Said Mom.

"GLADEEEEESE', Tap Tap Tap Tap Tap

He knew I was trying to study. Couldn't stand the fact that I'd graduated from high school, much less the fact of going to college. He'd magnify the nightly panorama until I'd storm out. The incessant, unrelenting bullshit was getting to me. I was determined to ignore him.

Tap Tap Tap Tap Tap," GLADEEEEEESE," Tap Tap Tap Tap Tap

Mom finally emerges from the kitchen drying her hands with the dish towel and snags the glass," Bastard." She barks then turned to me and said," You got some mail today.", reaching to the windowsill and handing me an envelope. I opened it and read it. It was my draft number. I had turned 18 just a couple weeks earlier. There wasn't much chance of being drafted. The war was slowing down. The last draft notices, the system coming to a halt, would be mailed December, 31, 1972. I put it in my pocket.

"WEELLLL?" Hands shuffling. "What da fuk I gotta do to get a fukin drink around here?"

She said, " I don't think you hafta worry about this." Handing it back.

"GODDAMMIT!" Rocking and shuffling up a storm.

I put on my jacket and strode out, I was taking Sunshine to the movies. We had become an item. Young lovers thrilled with life. Constantly holding hands and touching. We had done it.

It had been a beautiful autumn night, full moon, cool breeze blowing. I had pulled into the small park down the street from her house. We embraced, passions enflamed. We had touched each other before, establishing trust, but tonight we were going all the way. In urgent determination, not wise enough to get in the back seat, I took position in front of her. Sometimes, in passion, or in fear, one can exclude other sensations. It was magnificent, a personal revelation sharing an intimate, spiritual, and rite of passage with my friend and lover. But by the time we'd completed I had a circular brand on my right butt cheek from the consistent pressure on the cigarette lighter. Hurt like hell but it was worth it. Love and pain, Love and pain.

***

...and his heart was going like mad and yes I said yes I will yes. - James Joyce, *Ulysses*

***

January, 1973

" Hey Chief, you gotta live one here."

The Sergeant, a Marine, was smiling at me as I made my way toward the Navy desk. I heard a toilet flush and soon after an overweight man in whites, with anchors on his collar, came around the corner and had a seat. I was a surprise, he certainly didn't, considering the political climate, expect enlistees to walk right in.

Two nights earlier I had had a terrible row with Herman. I had had a dismal performance at the college. Inwardly I blamed him. I felt uncomfortable studying at the library but when I came home the nightly antics took their toll in my mind and in my grades. I had stormed out the apartment livid and somehow determined to get away. But I didn't have the money to move. As I reached into my jacket pocket for the car keys, out came the letter from the Draft Board. A well known verse repeated itself in the back of my mind for the next two days, ' Join the Navy and See the World.'

I took a series of tests which would establish an IQ which in turn would qualify me for certain rates, or jobs in the military. The Chief stressed that I would want a guarantee for an 'A' school after boot camp. He didn't want me to enter without a school. Otherwise I'd be a Boatswains Mate, or as he said," A Deck Ape." An unenviable position on any ship. But test results indicated I was eligible for the Alpha category of rates. I chose one and signed the contract to report for bootcamp in six months, the six months as incentive as time served for promotional reasons, and getting my affairs in order, prior to my first hitch. 4 years. 4 years of tears and more.

No man will be a sailor who has contrivance enough to get himself into a jail; for being in a ship is being in a jail, with the chance of being drowned. - Samuel Johnson, quoted in James Boswell's *The Life of Samuel Johnson.*

***

Humanism

"In Philosophy, attitude that emphasizes the dignity and worth of the individual. A basic premise of humanism is that people are rational beings who possess within themselves the capacity for truth and goodness. The term *humanism* is most often used to describe a literary and cultural movement that spread through western Europe in the 14th and 15th centuries. This Renaissance revival of Greek and Roman studies emphasized the value of the classics for their own sake rather than for their relevance to Christianity."

***

Sunshine wasn't happy. I hadn't discussed it with her. Should have, she was my partner after all. In lame explanation I pointed out that I didn't have to go until June. After she graduates from high school. We could make plans from there. Placated, though disappointed in my decision to put college on hold, we became even closer. I managed to pick her up from school and spend as much time with her as I could.

Mom wanted to get into the act. She knew I had found a love. I wanted to give Sunshine a token of my affection, and dedication. Mom offered to go to the Mall and help me pick out a ring. It was a small thing, with two hearts intertwined and small gem, but Mom thought it was reasonable and helped me pay for it. When I presented it to Sunshine she was pleased, glowing, she proudly displayed it to others. It seemed, at least for her, I was fulfilling what a man should do for his woman. She cried when I left for boot camp.

***

Proud to Serve

During his inaugural speech John F. Kennedy said,"Ask not what your country can do for you, ask what you can do for your country". In so saying, he espoused a concept that runs deep in our collective psyche, national service. A giving back, so to speak, for the freedoms and liberties we enjoy because of the efforts and sacrifices made by others. He made this statement in the aftermath of the Eisenhower years, a time of relative peace and tranquility that realized the most explosive economic growth the world had seen to date. Times were good and the future bright. Viet Nam was nowhere on the radar scope.

No other conflict, with the exception of the Civil War, has been more corrosive and divisive to our social character than the Viet Nam war. A famous journalist, noted for his battlefield exploits, reminisced by saying,"It was the wrong war, but for those who went, did so for the right reasons". By the time we extricated ourselves, in 1975, from this nightmarish battle, waged by politicians, with no clear mission except to contain the spread of communism, our national pride had been negatively affected leaving any thought of national service, much less military, an execrable endeavor. Yet, as time passes, and as we approach the year 2000, there is opportunity for renewal, within the framework of peace and prosperity, to once again consider some form of national service for our youth. Where they can experience a sense of pride and contribution, establish a bond, and serve to continue the legacy of freedom so nobly gained.

I feel that it is time for a resurgence. A time to instill a new direction. A time for reflection and discovery. Now, on the eve of a new millenium, we can reshape our focus, build from the inside and extend those precepts which we hold dear throughout the globe. Our concepts of freedom and equality, and the pride with which we share it, extended like a living hand to all. With such intensity so as to sway every theocracy, dictatorship, and dwindling communistic state to submit

I propose a national service. Compulsory. For a duration of two years. Whether military, industrial, overseas, or community. This service should be undertaken upon graduation from high school, and certainly for those who don't. Such service could be waivered for the college bound, but should be served as an internship upon reciept of a diploma.

I realize this is not a popular idea. It flies in the face of personal freedom; requiring indentured servancy without the consent of the individual; a fascist state dictating to it's youth; slave labor to be determined by unseeing bureaucrats. And who would pay for this service? Would there be increased taxes? Who determines who goes where? What good could come from this?

Much good could be derived from this endeavor.

Despite having the most sophisticated and powerful military in history, the manpower required to maintain this institution has dropped dramatically. Many regurgitate the old arguments of the wrong war, believing that those who serve are a lesser breed, even unable to make it in the outside world. An aged counter culture propaganda that fights any perpetuation of patriotism as maudlin; discipline as peurile; conformity as inherently evil. Treating with disdain the very people who enabled such a culture to exist.

Yet, I believe that many would gladly serve if given the opportunity, if nudged, to participate, if only for the experience and right to say they had. The right to having, in any small way, to have perpetuated a long, proud, and vital aspect of our society. The American Hammer.

As a retired member of the military family I can recite my own negatives against a stint, much less a career, in the armed forces. In many ways it can be a breeding ground for nepotism, favoritism, and abuse of power. Some have reached their status by virtue of time served, not any skill, effort, or inherent leadership. They tend to surround themselves with obsequious ingratiating sycophants who bob in unison. Skilled office politicians, lifeless drones without motivation or initiative who, through gossip and backstabbing, make themselves shine only by denigrating others. Such weak kneed leaders that promote appearance over performance create an atmosphere that erodes the work ethic and produces lethargic lackeys incapable of an independent thought much less initiative.

But there are positives as well if one is in the right environment. One learns to sacrifice for a greater ideal. Teamwork, pride, and humility become established values. One learns to endure hardship with dignity, make lasting friends that share a common bond. There is a building of mind and body along with an enhanced vision of the world that creates something our youth needs, self respect.

I recall when, after some time in the Gulf, our ship pulled into the port of Haifa, Israel. I went on an all day field trip in a bus that showed us the historical site of Masada and the unique Dead Sea. Sitting behind the bus driver I had a good view. A sparse country with not a lot of vegetation, it still had a beauty and ambience, a focal point in the history of mankind, that inspires cerebration. Due to delicate political considerations at the time we couldn't enter Jerusalem, but the driver did manage to take a road that overlooked the city. I didn't need to be reminded how volatile this small but important country is. The driver had a loaded pistol in his lap the whole trip

Legendary places capture the imagination. I still see myself looking out from the heights of Masada, down to the eroding ramp the Romans had built to storm the walls. One could still make out where the Romans had their encampments during the long siege. Masada, a physical reminder of defiance against overwhelming odds, and of sacrifice, denying the victors the satisfaction of living prisoners

That spirit was highlighted the next day. I and a shipmate decided to explore the city. Modern, with european overtones, it was thriving with many peoples of different nationalities, ethnicities, and beliefs. Eclectic.

We had decided, after an exhaustive walk, that it was time to take a break. We stopped at an outdoor cafe. Curiously enough we ordered hamburgers and fries. Upon taking a seat I noticed that it was late afternoon, and seated across from an urban thorougfare, looking down from a vantage point, I could observe many of the happenings of midcity traffic including pedestrian.

At first glance, people are people and buildings are buildings. At second glance they take shape. Commuters were returning home from their day's efforts. Small cars stopping at the light to let the walkers meet and pass each other in the boardwalk. Some white some dark, dressed in the latest fashions or traditional garb. Definitely another country but not so different as to make one feel out of place.

A bus pulled up. Through the windows, I could see passengers rise and line up for departure. A girl caught my eye, young and pretty. She had long brown hair in a pony tail. My gaze followed her movement to the front. I watched her confident air as she emerged to the sidewalk and purposefully marched down the street. She seemed so fragile and vulnerable, and yet not, with that huge rifle slung over her shoulder.

Many countries require service from their youth. Most under duress from their neighbors. But this service is a vital aspect of the national vision. Acclimating generations to their responsibilities, and, once completed, serving as reserve forces in defense of the homeland.

Envisioning future events, President Franklin Roosevelt signed the Selective Training and Service Act of 1940. It was the first peacetime draft. His foresight made the country more prepared for the years to come. From 1948 to 1973, in peace and war, the draft was utilized to fill gaps that could not be filled voluntarily. In 1975, due to the calamitous events of the Viet Nam war, registration was suspended. But it was prior to that, in 1973, that the draft had officially ended and we had an all volunteer military. Registration was reinitiated in 1980 by President Carter after the Soviets invaded Afghanistan. It continues today. It is estimated that of draft eligible youth, more than 93% comply with registering.

Those are awkward years, between 18 and 21. Many have no direction or guidance. Unless motivated through scholarship or supported by parents, a college degree is not a viable option. Rather than having these wayward souls roaming the streets or pidgeon hole themselves in occupations that serve no growth or development, why don't we provide some options?

President Kennedy sensed that, but with a broader vision. By launching the Peace Corps, he allowed individuals to travel and help others in need. Ambassadors expanding the principles which we cherish. Those who contributed returned home with a magnified view of the world and a sense of accomplishment. Could we create a version of the Peace Corps for our youth at home?

Let's face it. The Military is not for everyone. But it does provide skills and experiences one wouldn't recieve elsewhere. Skills that are translatable to the civilian sector. For those whom conscientiously desire not to serve their compulsory service in the military, let us offer other avenues.

State and community services could use the manpower. Closer ties with the government is the goal. Enable the youth to realize that they are a part of the system. Court systems, Police departments, Fire departments, community services, all could have a lasting beneficial effect, not only for the servicer but those institutions which recieve it In his "Farewell Address to the American People", President Ronald Reagan said:

An informed patriotism is what we want. And are we doing a good enough job teaching our children what America is and what she represents in the long history of the world? Those of us who are over 35 or so years of age grew up in a different America. We were taught, very directly, what it means to be an American. And we absorbed, almost in the air, a love of country and an appreciation of its institutions. If you didn't get these things from your family you got them from the neighborhood, from the father down the street who fought in Korea or the family who lost someone at Anzio. Or you could get a sense of patriotism from school. And if all else failed you could get a sense of patriotism from the popular culture. Movies celebrated democratic values and implicitly reinforced the idea that America was special (p.272).

I recieved my draft number in late 1972. I joined, voluntarily, in June 1973, with the United States Navy. I retired in 1995. During that time I witnessed the decline in prestige the military suffered during the post Viet Nam years and the deteriorating conditions of the Carter years. It was difficult not to be anti-establishment. Then there were the Reagan years.

Now is the time for a compulsory National Service. To expose our youth to the machinery of Freedom. Give them the experience in participating in something bigger than themselves. Instill that sense of altruism and charity in giving that is so much a part of our history. We need to remind ourselves and illuminate succeeding generations of their legacy. In his Address Ronald Reagan also said:

But now, we're about to enter the nineties, and some things have changed. Younger parents aren't sure that an unambivalent appreciation of America is the right thing to teach modern children. And as for those who create the popular culture, well grounded patriotism is no longer the style. Our spirit is back, but we haven't institutionalized it. We've got to do a better job of getting across that America is freedom-...And freedom is special and rare. It's fragile; it needs protection (p.272).

Works Cited

Casper, Scott E. and Davies, Richard O. Five Hundred Years: Exploring American

Traditions. Simon and Schuster, 1997.

http://www.sss.gov/backgr.htm. <u>Background of Selective Service</u>.

***

The Terrorist, that son of a bitch
May his peter be eaten by the 7 year itch
May his balls be beaten by the American Hammer
Till his asshole whistles the Star Spangled Banner

***

"LIBERTY CALL, LIBERTY CALL......LIBERTY CALL FOR DUTY SECTIONS ONE, THREE, AND FOUR........ NOW LIBERTY CALL"

Having cleaned the compartment with him a couple of times Spanky, as a good mentor, invited me to a party .Spanky felt, since I was working with Louie in the Captain's Office, that it would be good to get in good with me and invited me to a get together at a friends house.

After a breathtaking ride, Spanky drove his ancient white Comet like it was a Trans Am, we skidded in front of a dilapidated duplex. I could hear music blaring through the broken window from the household on the right. Gratefully, I followed Spanky to the left hand door. Without knocking he entered.

"Welcome to Twidget House.", He announced. I looked around. Though somewhat barren, the place seemed neat and well kept in keeping wth the inhabitants. The Twidgets were that group of ships company who worked above the waterline in the higher dominions either maintaining the electronics or facilitating operations for the officers. They were usually hush hush since most had security clearances. I had gotten to know most of them from my position in the CO's Office.

Suddenly there was a banging at the door. All heads turned as Bronco burst in. Bronco was one of five Boatswains Mates who lived next door. He said," Hey we're gettin reddy to go to that carnival across town. Dere's an arm wrestlin chimp dere who's never lost. We been gettin Bubba likkered up to take him down. Wanna go?" Spanky immediately said," HELL YEAH."

We all climbed into cars, Bronco and Bubba riding with us in the back seat. Bronco was a Second Class Bos'n and in his rate Second Class was godlike. Bos'n mates were the hardest workers on the ship. They were the Deck apes. He was tall, lanky, and knew his job being the Bos'n on the Captain's Gig. Though rough in manner, a learned trait, he was a leader and Bubba was one of his pupils. Bubba though, was a different story.

It was a joke that Bubba was a hillbilly from Bugtussel, in the hills some where. But in fact he came from the midwest some where. Somewhere bailing hay in his youth. He was huge, huge and burly, often being reminded to shave the dark curly hair from the back of his neck if only to prove he had a neck. And he was dumber than a box of hair.

We had steadily downed beers, Bronco bullying Bubba, when the Ferris Wheel came into view. I wondered how a little chimpanzee would overpower this walking fire hydrant. Passing the kiddy rides, rifle shoots, and Haunted House, we found ourselves staring into a round cage where a grey haired man with handlebar moustache exhorted any comers to take on his monkey.

He wasn't just any monkey, he was an Orangutan, and his name was Rufus, and he and his trainer had been together for twenty years. Whenever Handlebars would shout " Rufus" he would point his unused leather whip at him and the monkey would expose banana blackened teeth in a hideous grin. Dressed in black leather vest and shorts and seated across an oval table this monkey, one of the great apes, hadn't had many takers despite the enormous crowd.

151

Bronco said to Bubba," I got fifty bucks for the entry fee, whip his fukin ass and we'll split five hundred."

Bubba had always had a glazed look in his eyes. He was always called upon when manpower was the prerequisite and performed with Bronco's compliments. But even glazed eyes glazed by half a case of beer could see the size and depth of his opponent. He hesitated. Bronco said," You're not gonna pussy out on me are ya?"

Handlebars accepted the challenge and fee with a flourish. Bubba entered the cage. Handlebars directed Bubba to the seat opposite Rufus. But as he approached his seat it seemed he forgot it was an arm wrestling contest. Bubba charged Rufus and delivered a haymaker with all the force he could muster knocking Rufus off his stool sliding to the other side of the ring. Bubba turned to us with a big grin.

Few men would have risen from such a shot but Rufus was not a man. As Bubba gloated Rufus stood up on his knuckles, shook his head and glared at Bubba. Suddenly the apes shoulders began shaking and pumping up and down and an ear piercing howl erupted from the maddened creature. Bubba turned and his glazed eyes opened wide with clarity as the animal attacked. Bubba never made it to the gate. It took Handlebars and four staff members ten minutes to pull Rufus off.

Two weeks later, the very morning Bubba got out of the hospital, Captain's Mast was held. As a witness I was present when Bubba limped into the Captain's stateroom. A huge patch covered his left ear, his right arm was in a sling, and his face, neck, and shoulders were littered with scratches and bite marks. From that day forward Bubba had a new name, Cookie. Gorilla Cookie.

***

August, 1973

Boot Camp was easy, sort of, considering my background at Charlotte Hall. Balded heads, we would be rushed from one place to the other, indoctrinating procedures designed to instill discipline and team spirit. An eight week period that would, upon graduating, give a young sailor the knowledge, and pride, to commence his naval experience. It was during the fourth week I felt stressed. Sunshine wrote a letter that questioned our relationship, our Future. Commonly known as a 'Dear John' letter, I furiously wrote back of my continued loyalty and begged for her to wait until I returned. She was my Sunshine.

Mom and Pop picked me up at National Airport. Mom doted over me in my uniform, Herman seemed relieved. It was a quiet drive back until we came into the neighborhood. Mom became agitated. It seemed that a crime spree, murders, were being committed in the area. Wiping tears from her eyes she related to me that the Sherriffs, the Mom and Pop liquor store owners, had been killed early one morning, viciously, catching them after recieving a shipment. Also, a young black woman had been found murdered in her apartment. Rumour was there was three of them. Police were looking. I was shocked but not surprised knowing the neighborhood. I agreed with Mom how terrible it was but truthfully my mind was on seeing Sunshine.

To make things worse Peter was in prison. Seems he and another, the other got away, had abducted a young woman against her will and drove over state lines. Wally wanted to know if I wanted to join him for a visit. I said I would.

I hadn't been to a correctional facility since Uncle Dewey. Wally, carrying the obligatory chess set, here a pretense to respectability, led me to the visitors log. We endured a brief search, and, waiting for the barred door to open, entered the visiting room.

There was a U of tables, visitors to the outside, that stretched across an expansive theatre, plexiglassed stations in each corner with guards looking in. We sat at a table and waited. Soon Peter appeared in the barred entrance, the door opened, and beelined his way to our table.

We all hugged across the table. Small talk ensued. Peter listened, overly patiently, almost boringly, while I gave my accounts and aspirations. Wally had the chess set out and pieces placed. They started playing.

It was awkward sitting there watching them play, my gaze naturally spread around the room. We had come early but soon the room began filling up. The visitors were mostly women with children in tow, some by themselves, and a few men, like ourselves, brothers, fathers, and friends. Peter and Wally were checking the ladies out. I gleaned that having a woman on the outside was a point of manhood within the prison population. I could only imagine how tough it was in there.

Eyes scanned her when she walked in. Blonde haired, pinned back, with a tight red dress, she had taken time to impress. My awkwardness increased when she chose the seat next to me. Young and pretty, she smiled at me as she pulled the chair out. I smiled back and politely gazed back to the game.

Wally and Peter knew something. They were sharing knowing glances when he walked up to the table and sat opposite the Blonde. I couldn't help but look over, the whole room seemed fixated.

He was tall, blonde haired, and blue eyed. But something was wrong. His hair was braided in several pony tails, one dangling provocatively over his right eyebrow. Mascara, blue eye shadow, rouged cheeks, and red lipstick decorated his face. Opened shirt with tails tied suggestively below his belly button highlighted the feminine way he took his seat.

There was a tense silence. Both looked at each other. He said," What do YOU want?"

Suddenly and uncontrollably the pretty girl sitting beside me began crying. Inwardly cringing, sharing the young lady's grief, I was shocked to hear Peter and Wally laughing out loud. They laughed louder as she burst from the chair towards the exit.

***

Johnathan Swift (1667-1745) is the premier example of the bitter and sarcastic satirist.

Through his works such as <u>Gulliver's Travels</u> and <u>A Modest Proposal</u> he criticizes the powers that be, their morality, and their role in civilization.

In book 4 of <u>Gulliver's Travels</u>, Gulliver finds himself in the land of the Houyhmhms. A race of supremely intelligent and reasoning horses. He writes of the "Yahoos", a primitive form of human in the land. After learning their language he communicates the world across the water to the horses. He explains the causes of war, and the art of European Statecraft and law. The horses don't comprehend how sentient beings could behave like that, not as reasonable, thinking horses would. In the end, it is determined that he is too much like a Yahoo and must leave. Showing that even reasoning, intelligent horses must remove what is strange to them, not understandable, and disruptive to their culture. Racism?

In Book 3, he treats the new sciences and the concept of absolute rulers with satirical vigor. The King rules from a floating island that, scientifically, can be directed anywhere over the land. His analogy of an oppressive ruler covering the land in shadow is a reference to England and Ireland. The various scientists, so absorbed in their studies, to the exclusion of everything else, is an oblique aside to the new sciences. The King is eventually deposed. Tyranny, in the end, without compassion for the people, will never last.

In <u>A Modest Proposal</u>, an ironic attack on the policies of England and their stranglehold on the Irish, Swift proposes that since the Irish are so poor, a market for infant flesh be established. Those who could afford it could help in the economy of the lower class as well. Here he shows where reason is divored from ethics. Not to mention bitterly displaying the plight of the poor and the deaf ears of the government. This work is a bitter attack on that facet of human nature to oppress and enslave.

Swift is a misanthropist. This viewpoint is based on his innate sense of man's nature. One that appears to entertain selfishness, apathy, cruelty, and class distinctions without embracing the true precepts of religion or altruism.

Though both authors are enlightened visionaries. Men of thought and reason. They convey through their works that side of human nature that prevents us from growth and development. Our selfishness and greed for power and wealth, the lack of compassion for our fellow beings. Yet to strive for knowledge and pursue it with intellectual curiosity should be the object lesson, to treat others with the same equanimity we treat ourselves.

Both men of letters, one striving under the shadow of the middle ages, the other, the oppression of England. Each though sensitive and understanding of human nature, rails against those aspects of our character that prevent us from our true potential. Both though learned, are hardened and inured to their own demons and philosophical enemies.

Marlowes day, without doubt, was violent and crude. But to sense man's true nature, he must have lived with zest and vigor. Much like an Ernest Hemingway, a man's man despite a sensitive and discerning disposition. A contemporary of Shakespeare, his musings and literary works might have been as much an influence on western civilization if not for an early death in a bar fight. Contempt for those less gifted or erudite must have surely been a part of his nature.

Swift knew death was inevitable. A religious man, he must have dwelled upon heaven and earth with ferocious sincerity. His feelings for the less fortunate and the desperate poverty of those confined without hope is displayed in his writings and his own epitaph. Written in latin , composed himself, it reads,"He has gone where savage indignation can lacerate his heart no more."

All of us have the faculties to assess our world and make judgements, flavored by our own experiences and academic upbringing. We each have the need and desire for growth and development within the confines of our conscience and hopes. Each man individually, seeks his own personal goals and sometimes forgets the aspirations of others and in turn considers others, as a group, the enemy.

In a letter to Alexander Pope, dated September, 29 ,1725, Swift wrote," I have ever hated all nations, professions, and communities, and all my love is toward individuals...But I principally hate that animal called man...Upon this great foundation of misanthropy...I will never have peace until all honest men are of my opinion."

***

' Men fear death, as children fear to go in the dark; and as that natural fear in children is increased with tales, so is the other. ' - Francis Bacon, *Essays*.

August, 1973

There were three of them.

Sunshine had gotten a new car, it wasn't new it was her first. She, like I had, was entering a new phase in life, Freedom. She took pride in driving me around town. Her Sailor just back from Bootcamp. I was proud of her. We were equals. She was still wearing my ring. We were still partners. I still loved her. She still loved me.(It's daylight now, I sense the sun through blinds I've never opened.)

It was a warm autumn night. No moon, only the stars twinkling. Sunshine had picked me up for a night at the movies. She drove that little Toyota with authority and confidence. When we reentered the castle grounds I convinced her to park at the other end, facing The Woods. I began necking and nadoodling her. I was passionate.

In the midst of my fury I noticed a small yellow car had stopped nearby. Considered another member of the castle grounds I continued my assault. I never heard them.

Sunshine tensed. I looked up to see a dark man with a gun to her head. A noise forced my gaze to the right and I looked directly into the barrel of another gun. The barrel was framed by a white, yellowish face topped by a white woolen cap. The door opened and he said,"Get out." For the second time in my life I felt fear.

I obeyed. At the same time I heard the other man say," Take your pants off." Sunshine obeyed. The yellowish man told me to empty my pockets out on the roof of the car. I obeyed. Sunshine was told to get in the back seat. She obeyed. Yellow grabbed me by the back of the collar and directed me to the curb and said," Down." I obeyed. I heard Sunshine make a sound. I jerked and felt the barrel of a gun slapped to the back of my head,"Don't move." I obeyed. I laid there, shaking and shrinking inside, while they took turns on her. Quivering with anger and fear, the back of my mind told me I had seen that yellowish face before. Before. Before....

I had closed so much inside I never heard them leave. Time had passed. Inured to my nose to the ground I heard,"Bobby?" I looked up and saw Sunshine adjusting her halter top in the passenger seat. I rose, hands spread in supplication. She said," Please drive me home." I did. Driving down Landover Road I looked to the left and saw a small yellow car parked in front of the 7-11. Anger rose inside and I said, " That's them", and put on the turn signal. Sunshine said, " NO...NO... Please don't Bobby please don't Please just drive me home....PLEASE." I saw the fear and pain in her eyes. I turned back into the traffic. One week later I reported for duty branded in mind and spirit. I didn't see Sunshine for a long time after. She had given herself for our lives. The shock, the pain, and the anguish worked its way into my being from that moment on. More than innocence was lost that night.

***

Stardust. We are all Stardust. Recent discoveries, most notably from the Hubble telescope, demonstrate the vast periods of time which we, as individuals, find incomprehensible. The birth and death of stars might be considered within the space of one sentence, but the time between unchaptered. We, God's children, need to acclimate our past, note our origins, and look towards the future. Because we, in time, are the eyes of the universe.

***

Marx and Darwin: Concepts of Change

The fabric of history is replete with colorful characters who define, bring depth, and dimension to the tapestry of time. Many share common characteristics in their contributions. Men like Alexander, Ghengis Khan, Cortes, and Napoleon colored this tapestry through conquest and dominion. But there are those who changed the entire weave and did so by the power of thought; Plato, Aristotle, and Galileo. Looking back, we can see the growth and development of civilization by the passage of time. Fortuitous events, ideological movements, and natural disasters have made their impression. The evolution of man and culture, both biologically and socially, and how change occurs within each have been the visions, in thought, of two of the most influencial scholars of the 19th century, Marx and Darwin. Both men challenged the system and set in motion fundamental changes in how we view the world, one in the shifting sands of economics and the natural transition to communism, the other disputing the long held beliefs of the religious community. Change, to Marx and Darwin, occurs without conscious planning or effort, somewhat capricious with regard to Darwin, less so with Marx.. Marx sees economic circumstances that determine change, Darwin, "Natural Selection" in evolution. Both set in motion new forces, new ideologies that have changed history forever.

Karl Marx wrote in <u>The Communist Manifesto</u> that "The forces of change are in the interstices"(cracks). Trained in economics and part of the aristocracy, he was perfectly positioned to observe how industry and society operated and functioned. He saw different modes of production such as feudal, capitalist, and communist.

Marx describes how economics was the driving force in civilization's change from feudalism to capitalism. Feudalism had been a stable system for centuries. Goods were produced for use rather than exchange. Traditionally, the Lord of the Manor was the law, and the serfs who worked the land obeyed this law and served their Lord as a duty, swearing allegiance. The growth of industry and a market exchange in the 16th and 17th centuries, caused a sharp increase in population in major cities and a decline in rural commmunities. As new inventions created surplus goods, a buyer and seller environment emerged, where profit for the seller became a means of income. Thus Capitalism was borne, and with it a greater disparity in classes and wealth.

He notes that there are two kinds of revolution (i.e. change), political and economic. Using the French Revolution as an example of political change it is examined that the Bourgeoisie, a minority, initiated the revolt against the Aristocracy. This movement was bloody and chaotic. But an economic revolution would be widespread and deeply rooted, therefore bloodless and easily transitioned.

Describing historical change, he postulates that there is a thesis, argument, or ideology. This state is stable until an anti-thesis emerges, wherein, from confrontation or compromise, a synthesis is formed. This synthesis becomes the thesis, and so on. With this in mind, Marx determined that capitalism would worsen and decay, and be synthesized into Communism

It was never envisioned that a semi-feudal state like Russia would become the standard bearer for Communism. It should have been a more affluent country for his principles to come to fruition. We know now that Communism is a dwindling ideology. Yet time marches on, and with it the possibility of a purer transition may develop. His concepts have not been completely disproven, or proven, but change, without conscious planning or direction, seems a solid theory for now

***

Charles Darwin published <u>The Origin of Species</u> in 1859. And with it caused a paradigm shift in modern scientific thought and observation. The primary theory he proposed was that all creatures were subject to change through evolution and that the change would come about by a process called "Natural Selection". Each creature dependent on survival within its environment, "Survival of the Fittest", would acquire certain characteristics that enabled reproductive growth and food acquisition. These characteristics would be passed on to the offspring. Thus change would occur from one species to another. The individual most adapted to its environment would be most likely to perpetuate. There are variations within each individual in each species. Those variations that are the most favorable to adaptation have the most chances to be preserved. But this is a random process in that adaptations to the environment are not necessarily growth and development, and not considered absolute in evolving a higher species

The difficulty in establishing this theory was the concept of the enormous amount of time involved. Without the benefit of Mendel's Laws of Inheritance (1866), and not generally accepted until the turn of the century, Darwin was in disputation with the dominant forces of societal thought, namely "The Church". Time has consistently supported his theory through the archeological record and is now considered foundational. It is his concept of "Natural Selection" that creates change, a random process that like Marx's cannot be planned or directed, but change will occur.

Summary

For fifteen centuries, until Galileo proved Copernicus right, the theological and intellectual communities adhered to the geocentric faith of Earth as the center of the universe. I believe it was during this time that the "Church", under stress from discoveries of the New World, Martin Luther, and the new sciences contending with the Platonic/Aristotelian world, reacted with zeal against any opposition to their faith The struggle between science and religion has continued to this day. Intrepid men, armed with the secular truths of science forcing believers to reconcile the fictions of faith to the facts of life.

Neither Marx nor Darwin mention God in their works. Each, within his own profession, builds upon the sciences and the history of man. One can sense an irreversible progression in how man views himself since the ancient Greeks. It seems that they were both observing change within their respective sciences, historical change in societal conditions, and evolutionary change through climactic and environmental adaptations. Each appears to be correct. Change cannot be planned or directed, not even a predicted outcome. But a change in economics dictates a change in society, and the process of "Natural Selection" is as natural as the seasons.

Marx envisioned a bloodless revolution. One where the masses simply assume control. An educated middle class, evolutionarily, both physically and socially, equals. This may yet come to happen. Semi-feudal economies like Russia and China were not the ideals. Their experiment with communism was, and is, bloody and ruthless.

If Marx and Darwin consider change inevitable what are the possible outcomes? As Europe is consolidating towards a single currency, Asia with its cheap labor, and Nafta binds the Americas, we come closer to a world economy that may best fit Marx's qualities for that bloodless transition. And, if genes that more suit the adaptation of humans to computers in the "information age" come to dominate in succeeding generations, we may all look less differentiated physically, with commonalities in both social, spiritual, and demographic arenas. But as we change and merge, one people, one economy, one class, what change will happen then? Individuality? Changing ideologies? The mercurial nature of man dictates change, both as Darwin's evolutionary animal and as Marx's shifting economic circumstances of materialism intertwine and create yet another weave to the tapestry. Thesis, anti-thesis, synthesis.

***

1984

I groaned when he said it. I looked at the other two guys and they kinda shrugged. We were going to do it anyway, but I knew he had used that line before. We followed him to the tailor shop. No self respecting American Sailor visits Hong Kong without buying a suit or two. It was just that we wanted to hit the bars first, that's all.

Hong Kong. Enclave of British Colonialism, where east meets west. A cultural syncretism of western values and eastern tradition. Funny how all I seem to remember is our guide and the Red Lips Bar.

The Red Lips Bar. After a couple of days we had hit most of the bars on the mainland and decided to take the ferry to Kowloon. Checking out the shops looking for deals it soon became a burden muscling through the throngs of people. Glancing down an alleyway I saw a sign hung over a door. The sign was a picture of red lips with one word in English beneath, 'BAR'.

Parting thick green drapes designed to fend off sunlight we entered. Standing there waiting for our eyes to adjust to the darkness we heard the welcoming voices of the bargirls and gentle hands leading us to the bar. Ordering beers and shots we turned to gaze at our escorts. There were six of them and three of us and, with the exception of the bartender, we were the only people in the house. Moments passed before I realized that with uncanny skill I had led us to the one place that employed the oldest bargirls in the Orient. The youngest had to be eligible for Social Security.

Bending to the pleas and unable, or unwilling, to be selective, we donated to the juke box and bought each of them a drink. It was how they made a living and I, for one, felt a tug at the heart for these matriarchs. Each of whom, true to the sign, were heavily painted with makeup and red red lips.

I soon found humor with the situation. At first it was repulsive the way they rubbed against us and flirted suggestively. I started the dialogue of asking how many grandchildren, and in a couple cases, great grandchildren they had. After a few more rounds we were laughing hilariously at each other. A few more and we were dancing. By the end of the evening slow dancing in the fragile embrace of those wise in years yet young at heart. We barely made it back to the last ferry.

Scrambling across the brow we were the last to board. Leaning against each other we found a wooden bench and dropped directly across from two Buddhist Nuns, one old, one young. Giggling, faces festooned with the red red lips mementos of grateful Grannies, I noticed the younger nun bending the ear of the older, her gaze never wavering from us. Halfway across the channel one shipmate, suddenly noticing he was seaborne, jumped up with hand clamped over his mouth and dashed to the rail emptying his stomach with audible clarity. I can still hear the young nun, voice rising in intensity, the older suffering the onslaught. I can only imagine what she was saying.

The day before departure I went to the tailor shop to pick up my suits. There was our guide. He assured me that I would be pleased with my suits, it seems he recieved a fee for every customer he delivered. It was hard to look at him. It was obvious he had been on the losing end of a knife fight. A deep vivid scar stretched in a straight line from his left cheek, across his nose, and ended parting his right eyebrow. I wondered how many times he had met sailors at the docks and convinced the reluctant by saying," Eef I no bring customer, I lose face!"

***

Explication of Artifact: The Compass in Chinese Navigation

Knowledge of Magnetite, or lodestone, has been documented in Chinese literature as early as the 4th century. The mysterious properties of lodestone became fundamental to the cult practice of Geomancy which permeated society for many centuries. It was not until the 10th century that mariners began to utilize magnetized needles in the form of a compass in assisting navigation. Long before Europe, the Chinese used floating wooden fish shaped objects containing lodestone, fish shaped iron or steel magnets, and pivoted wooden turtle shaped objects with lodestone. In a document written between 1111 and 1117, Chu Yu, son of a high official at Canton, describes a merchant expedition "... ship's pilots are acquainted with the configurations of the coasts; at night they steer by the stars, and in the daytime by the sun. In dark weather they look at the south pointing needle".

Throughout history, Chinese technology has equaled or surpassed that of Europe. The Axil age, Socrates, Confucius, and Buddha, demonstrated that humankind maintained parity in moral, scholarly, and religious pursuits independently. How would world events have changed if Chinese mariners expanded their routes before the Europeans? A Chinese enclave might have been established in England by the name of Hong Kong. Not impossible considering that Chu Yu depicted the compass almost a century before it was documented in Europe.

***

Halftime, and things weren't looking good. We had evened up in wins but in points, balls made, we were behind. Pondering strategies I noticed the Reverend take a seat at the bar. I made my way to his chair.

As I approached, his wings came into view. It was a marvelous sight. They were pearlish white with golden overtones and streaks of orange and green rippled their length. Remembering the garish colors of the Conquistadors I suddenly asked the Reverend, " Why is there good and evil in the world?"

He turned his sapient eyes towards me and said, " That is a question humanity has attempted to answer since the beginning. For a long time there was a school of thought called The Chain of Being. For many this concept explained the presence of evil in the world. Evil in the absence of good. There were three principles, Plenitude, wherein the universe is full, that is, filled with all possible existences, Continuity, that with all possible forms each shares at least one commonality with another, and Linear Gradation, in which all things range in order from the most primitive form of existence to the *ens perfectissimum,* the most perfect being, the one from whom all others come from, God. The goodness of the universe as a whole would be in its fullness and the best world the greatest variety of beings and therefore the same varieties of evil."

Sugar was motioning that it was my game next so I said," So within that gradation thing, where do we stand?" And he said, being the Reverend he is," From my understandings it appears we range somewhere below Angels." I smiled and rose towards the table. My smile disappeared when I saw Garr.

Without reaching into his pocket for a quarter Garr said," Heads." I pulled out a quarter, flipped it onto the table and said," Tails, your rack." Garr, their captain, gruffly pulled out the change, punched it in, and as he strode to the end of the table to rack said," I've been looking for you. I think you owe me one."

I walked back to the NADS table where Dexter had joined Cherrie, Fancy, and Sugar. I noticed that Cherrie's wings had seemed to grow, colors growing in intensity. Sugar said." Don't let him talk to you, that's half his game." Fancy said," Get him." And Cherrie, with a forcefulness she hadn't shown since her return

167

said," I wanna nother shot, I need it." She grabbed my hand and squeezed. I saw the pain of a new beginning. I nodded.

Something inside began burning. Garr and Turk watched my approach to the table. I bent to take aim. The thought of good and evil entered my being. I broke the ball with all my force and stood amazed as the cue ball curved off the lead ball, hit the two corner rails, and banged the eight ball right into the side pocket. The bar erupted with GO-NADS, GO-NADS, GO-NADS. I turned to Garr and said," Maybe next time."

Though my immediate win was room for elation we were still behind in points. In reversing our rotation the last game would be Cherrie and Turk again. My win had kept us alive but Turk only had to make one ball to win.

The Conquistadores were having a quarrel. Despite her absence Cherrie's reputation was still in effect. We could hear Turk's team urge him not to break the balls out. In his arrogance he strode to the table, bent to his task, and thundered the racked balls to all corners of the table. He hadn't made anything. It was Cherrie's turn.

Cherrie approached the table. Her wings were a rigid dark cobalt blue, tense and focused. The first three balls were automatic. Her fourth she played off one of his in the side and spanked it so well to break out the rest of her balls. Addressing the game and match winning shot she said," Side Pocket." and shot it in with a firm but feminine force.

The house roared. Cherrie turned and ran into the arms of Dexter. Sugar, Fancy, and I hugged and danced as our friends screamed in celebration.

In the tumult I saw Turk turn away from the table. His reddened face shrouded hate filled eyes and as he faced his angered colleagues I saw that his wings had become blackened husks pulsing with shame.

> Hell hath no limits, nor is circumscribed
> In one self place, for where we are is hell,

And where hell is there must we ever be.
- Christopher Marlowe, *Doctor Faustus*

***

August, 1988

Every Sunday, whenever in port anywhere in the world, I called home to Mom. For the last two years I had had overseas shore duty. Normally it was a three year billet but I had requested a transfer to sea duty a year earlier specifying orders to the east coast. I wanted to be close to home, Mom's health was deteriorating. Her liver was going.

A week before my return home I called Mom. She was excited. I knew she was lonely in the house by herself. It was a nice brick three bedroom with a basement in a middle class neighborhood. She and Herman had moved in while I was on my first Med cruise. At least I didn't have to see the castle or The Woods anymore. As usual we discussed the family. Most often the boys, Peter and Wally.

My homecoming was timely, Peter was getting out of prison again. Mom broke the news that the day he was to be emancipated he was to be married, again. We marveled over how he seemed to gain the affections of a woman from behind bars, again. It seemed that his good looks and charm should have been mitigated by the reasons he had spent so much time in jail. So many years over the abuse of women, again and again.

Mom met me at the door dragging my seabag. We had done this many times before. She was home. She was the only one who had seen the changes in me, the only one who understood and knew me.

The first time I had seen the house was after my first Med cruise. Somewhat of a joke with the guys when your family moves on you while you're away. Though Mom had always wanted a house it seemed that I was in mind as well. A fresh start for all.

But with my return I found that my other Brothers of the Woods had become statistics, aspects of humanity, as well. Of just the five of us caught in The Woods, one had shot the other in the chest and killed him over a can of beer, another was selling his body to men in downtown D.C.. Every homecoming seemed special in its own way.

But this homecoming was my last with Mom. Young men, or at least this young man, fevered in the prime of youth, tended not to appreciate what he had until it was gone. She was my touchstone, my confidante, and yet not. I had erected emotional barriers she was not allowed to bridge. Sunshine and my view of myself.

Self perception has different mirrors. One of mine was in the basement. Here were my accumulations of the years. A rug from Florence, fur from England, furniture and stereo from Japan, a white couch, childhood mementos and decades spanning clothes. It was here I would spend my quiet moments. It was here I sensed the passage of time.

Granted with acne shortly after 'A' school, from which I graduated first in my class, I found the years had taken its toll on a once clear complected and boyish face. Therefore it was a simple routine procedure to shower, shave, and slap on a set of service whites for the wedding ignoring, or rationalizing, a deep pain that had materialized in ones most common expression, one's face.

Vanity, and its pain, seems hereditary. Impatient with Mom's endeavors in the bathroom I walked in and stood behind her as she applied makeup. I looked at her as she looked at herself in the mirror. There is no such thing as perfect human symmetry. The face we see in the mirror is not the face others see. In the mirror I saw the face my mother had seen, since youth, grow old and gray. The look was the same yet different, backwards, or reversed. One eye and eyebrow slightly higher than the other, unnoticed till now, freckles on the other cheek, the ready grin warped to the other side as I tickled her. But as she turned to kiss me I saw the mirror of love I had seen all my life. The only accurate look of ourselves, it seems, is in the eyes of others.

Following directions we pulled up to a well kept single story house in suburban Virginia. The house belonged to a friend of the Bride. I knocked. The Bride to Be answered and led us through to the backyard where an arch of flowers had been erected, the altar for the vows.

The future Mrs.Peter was surprisingly articulate and sophisticated despite the heavy accent. Mom and I accepted her immediately. She was just what Peter needed. I hoped it would work out but his track record was dismal. We all sat down and chatted and waited. Wally would be bringing Peter directly from the Prison.

Wally and Peter pulled up in a small blue truck. During his incarceration Peter had been one of the fortunates to secure a paying job. He then turned his paychecks, pitiful as they were, over to Wally who, unbelievably enough, had gained employment as a security officer at the same institution. It's unknown all the mischiefs these two may have committed in their lives but in my minds eye they could have traded places and no one would have known the difference. Through Wally, the truck was the result of Peter's efforts.

I have often envied others with brothers and sisters. I can only imagine sharing the discoveries of youth with a sibling. Mine were in name only. But Peter and Wally had had each other, and their experiences, including Herman and the Boys Home, had created a bond that included a tense unvoiced rivalry. They had spent their lives jabbing each other in the ribs with military issue knives, their's was a hateful love. Mom and I knew that.

I know there is truth that you can find a good woman in church. In the early years Peter had taken me to church with one of his women. I recall how he feigned a spiritual lifestyle, even fancied himself a carpenter, Jesus' trade. We filed into a middle pew, and, sitting between us, after singing loudly, settled into calm repose with eyes clamped to the words of the pastor. A few minutes passed. The smell semed to come from the abyss of hell. His girlfriend placed her hand over her mouth and nose. I began waving the hymnbook surreptitiously. The family of parishioners directly in front were visibly upset, not to mention the groans of those behind us. That's when he started snoring. Disdain has never been more nobly represented, in view of a full church, than by the ability to fart and snore at the same time.

The wedding was brief. After the vows there was a brief reception in the house. Mom and I took station in a corner and observed. Peter displayed the charm and grace I'd always known him for, treating his new Bride with gentle respect. All thought that this was an uncommonly special union. The newlyweds thanked all and loaded themselves into the blue pickup waving as they pulled away. The rehabilitated tools of a carpenter in the back bed. Mom, my muse and mentor, not to mention my sense of humor, whispered," She's a beautiful girl, I just never thought I'd have an immigrant as a daughter-in-law."

***

The stranger seemed so familiar. Usually Smitty's was barren on Monday afternoons so I'd come over and get a roll of quarters from Lizzie and practice on the table. After a couple of games by myself I noticed the stranger sitting in the corner brooding darkly into his beer. His eyes met mine and we nodded. It suddenly seemed that I was looking at a younger version of myself.

He was about due to retire from the Navy. Another year I think he said. His eyes reflected a conscious past. His voice carried a boyish quality married to intelligence. Somehow I knew I could trust him. He offered to play a game and I acceded. With a boyish smile he said," For a drink?", I nodded back with a smile and watched as he racked the balls.

White tennis shoes, levi jeans, and clean shirt coupled with smooth confident movements, I sensed a challenge. As he strode past to select a cue from the wall rack his wings came into view.

They were broad and waved gently. Under the light I could see the feathers laced with a light blue at the tips gathering strength to a cold dark blue green, a sad grey at the stems. But where the feathers reached to the neck there seemed to be a confusion of colors, a battle of thoughts. As he reached for a stick his wings slowly spread and I could see a difference in the right wing. It was as if it had once been broken, long ago, and not quite healed back to its original shape.

After several games we had broken even and I suggested we take a break. I said," Whadya gonna do after the Navy?", and he said," Well, I'm not sure yet, except for the fact of taking about a year off....After that I expect to go to school on my G.I. Bill." I saw Sugar , Candy and Fancy coming through the front door, smiling, I said to the stranger, " What's your plans after that?". And he said," I'm not sure, I remember an Aunt, noting my discontent with the military about ten years ago, asked me what I really wanted to do in life...... I had no answer. So she said if you don't know what you wanna do.... just start making a list of those things you don't wanna do. Smart Lady." Then, looking me straight in the eye, he said," a higher education has been my goal for some time, just to prove I can." In the honesty of his eyes I saw conviction, but I also sensed the hidden pain of a broken wing. I rose to greet my friends and when I turned to introduce them to a unique man he was gone.

Momentarily confused I quickly recovered and pulled a chair out for Fancy. She seemed especially jubilant, her wings pulsing in baby blue and a rosy pink. I ordered a round from Lizzie.

I guess I hadn't noticed. Fancy stood up and turned to me with a couple of quarters in her hand and said," Play a game?." She was radiant with white high heeled pumps, red hip hugging jeans, and white satin blouse. On her lapel was a small turtle with white spots painted on the shell. I looked into her smiling eyes and said," Please."

***

1983

After two hours of riding the trains I found myself waiting behind the customs barricade at the Tokyo International Airport. Her flight had come in. Anxiety increased as I saw people queue into the stalls and she not in sight. Suddenly there she was checking her bags at a counter. Head and shoulders above her inspector. Regal, confident, cosmopolitan, fearless.

I was thrilled. My life's love had come back to me. Ten years later our love had still endured. On my part the intervening years had been spent living a sailors life, unhooked and rootless. She was my anchor, my future, my past. And most important, I was still a part of her heart. On her part she had taken years of therapy and became the first of her family to become a college graduate. Magna Cum Laude. No fool she. Proud man I.

But the years between 18 and 28, within our minds, became worlds apart. Despite our love it became clear our philosophies had changed. We had each evolved and adapted within our environments to an inimical world. She, supported by a loving and caring family, had charged ahead immersing herself into the world of higher knowledge. And I, inured to a structured lifesyle through Charlotte Hall, had become adept to the military environment. But in fact the chasm between us was far greater. Through force of thought, rationalization, and endeavor she was a victim no longer but a mindful personality, warm and magnetic. In contrast I had languished. Victimized by the belief that I had failed in protecting her virtue I had embraced the stereotypical concept of the wayward sailor, couching my fears and insecurities behind a veil of alcohol. False manhood, puffed chest, and insincere bravado had become my trademarks. Early on I knew she had become a much better person than I. Smarter, much smarter.

She knew something I didn't. Unsheltered minds normally do. Especially those who've challenged the halls of academia and emerged with alacrity. Our arguments had not centered on who left the top off of the toothpaste but on world matters, concepts, and beliefs. She would speculate how things should be and I, in ignorance, would stipulate how things are. Her optimism and my pessimism were incompatible. She had learned to approach the world with an enlightened vision, and I still saw things in black and white.

I don't remember the exact words, yet I knew she was right, when she commented how the educated shared less in common with those less used to books. Once the pretense of a macho demeanor had been exposed she recognized I was still the little boy, face to the curb, shaking in fear. She had conquered where I had not. Girl no longer, Lady. Woman.

Once the decision had been made there was no argument. She had plans in life and I had accepted an indentured servancy. I walked her to the bus and watched as she took a seat on my side. As the bus moved she waved and I saw her begin to cry. I know she was crying for me. A better woman will never exist.

Parting is all we know of heaven.
And all we need of hell.
- Emily Dickenson, " My life closed twice before its close"

***

" RELIEVE THE WATCH

0745

I had already relieved the Officer of the Deck fifteen minutes earlier. The senior men should always set the example. I watched as the Petty Officer of the Watch and the Messenger were relieved. The oncoming and offgoing POOW's both turned to me, saluted, the oncoming saying," I have the Watch." I returned the salutes.

Just then I heard a body moving up the brow. I turned to greet the newcomer to my ship, officially appointed to monitor all movement across the quarterdeck. I saw a new recruit dragging his seabag. He stopped at the foot of the brow holding his brand new ID card in his left hand as taught, saluted the flag at the stern, turned to me, saluted and said," Permission to come aboard Sir." I couldn't help but smile and said, " Welcome aboard."

It ocurred to me that over the years I had seen a sea of faces. Each ship I had served with had been a world unto itself. Each member, from the Commanding Officer to the lowest recruit had both rights and responsibilities. Each , regardless of background, served a common purpose and each, in time, were replaced to maintain the mission of the ship. Plenitude, Continuity, Linear Gradation.

I directed the new recruit to the POOW in order to facilitate his introduction to his new bosses when the oncoming and offgoing Messengers approached. They both saluted and I heard, saw, and felt the oncoming Messenger say," I,I,I, re re re relieve the the the Wa Wa Wa Watch." Oh God.

***

1988

It was our last laugh. There is nothing , within human culture, that is more profoundly influential to ones personal being than a mothers love. Without it a vacuum exists, culturally speaking, and certainly for men, where the nurturing side of life creates a veneration and respect for the opposite sex. I've seen what happens when that aspect is missing, generally absent, or ineffectual. When I turn to the memory of my own mother I smile. There is a bond, a shared concept of the world that time and space will never erase.

We had been laughing since the day after the wedding. Every time she would say, " Poor thing.", we'd crack up. I had heard her say it for years, whether it was an orphaned child, beleaguered adult, or suffering animal her first response would be, " Poor thing." And she said it with conviction, sincerely acknowledging the subjects misfortune and their plight in life. She cared and, if able, offered help and condolences.

The phone rang and Mom answered. After a few moments I heard her say," Poor thing." Hanging up the phone she silently sat shaking her head and said," After all those years behind bars he just can't get an even break." I said, " What's the matter?" She rose to take a drink from the glass kept by the fridge," That new truck Wally got Peter broke down..... the transmission went.....seems it can't be fixed. And Wally refuses to take responsibility for it. I guess he said ' tough shit '." Mom moved back to her seat and said," Poor thing." As we looked at each other the hilarity began to bubble up. In moments we were laughing so hard we had to hold on to each other to keep from falling down. In this family, a lack of sympathy was a tradition for the emancipated.

The car was loaded and I was ready to go. Time for me to report to my new duty station. I would have a couple of months of training in Norfolk so I'd be home every other weekend or so. We sat at the kitchen counter in silence. I was still licking wounds from an all night bender, Mom engaged with her crosswords.

" Well I should be on my way, I'd like to be there before dark." Really envisioning revisiting the nightlife down there. " Well okay, I hate to see you go.", Mom said, walking me to the door. Straightening my collar she said," I'd sure like to see you find a young lady.....do you ever talk to Sunshine anymore?" I stiffened at the question," No Mom, I guess we kinda grew away from each other (I thought,' Yeah, she's a matured college graduate, I'm still a drunk.'), but don't worry, I'll find a young lady one of these days." We kissed. As I pulled out of the driveway she stood at the door waving and lip synching, " POOR THING." We grinned at each other as I cruised away. It was my final image of her alive.

***

A good bartender is a good bartender. They're usually in your neighborhood bar. They've seen the world through the eyes of others and know the pulse of the neighborhood. The fears, pains, celebrations, and needs of their charges are dealt with with equanimity. A patient ear and cheerful tongue are tools of the trade.

Lizzie was in her element. The afternoon crowd had become loud and brisk. She bounced from one end of the bar to the other granting her elementary smile, wink, and word spreading laughs and goodwill in her wake.

Sitting at the end of an oval bar I viewed her wings in action. Soft and tender with the lonely, wary confidence with the stranger, flirtatious with the painters, professional with the professionals. She saw I needed a refill and glided my way. Our eyes met. I said," How do you do it?". And Lizzie said, " Love like you've never been hurt, work like you don't need the money, dance as if nobody's watching, sing like no one is listening, and live like it's Heaven on Earth." She smiled, winked, and laughed her way to the other end of the bar. Her wings were beaming.

***

" The mind of man is capable of anything - because everything is in it, all the past as well as all the future." Joseph Conrad, *Heart of Darkness*

The years have passed. Still, I remember some things. I remember the first time I felt fear. I remember the first and second times I smoked a cigar. I remember the glorious year of my first love and the second time I felt fear. I remember family and friends, the times good and bad. I remember military school and subsequent career. I remember when I kissed Mom twice one morning and our last laugh, but I don't seem to be able to remember myself as I would have myself remembered or know myself now as I would remember myself to have been.

I'd forgotten I had it. Rummaging in my briefcase I came across the only picture of myself other than ID and Driver's license. I recall when it was taken. My Bootcamp picture. A young sailor in the bloom of youth, unpebbled face, ready to see the world with a pure heart, proud soul, and clean conscience. I can still feel the eagerness, the wonderment, the joy of life. It's not the face I see in the mirror. It's the vision of a young mind unfettered, a clean slate unchiseled. Tabula Rasa.

YOUNGER ME, LISTEN UP. With time comes change, we are a mutable species. We've become not the you you remember. That glorious summer day we sent that message, we made it before the definitions of destiny were defined. And we have become a reflection of defining moments.

Universities are the heartbeat of civilization. Year after year they pulse new minds into society. Knowledge, the bricks of society, are passed down generation to generation for new minds to build with. Old or young, higher knowledge enables a vision for the future, and, in some cases, the past. But knowledge, to soothe if not remove deepest pains, takes time to fill the interstices of the soul.

Younger me whadya think? Lets end this cycle of self-destruction. In the autumn of our life let us shed the leaves of yesteryear and reach naked limbs to the sky. We have suffered the long winter's night and its time to begin again. There's more of the world to see, more to learn, more people to meet. We may come to see that, in time, we all see changes in our schools of thought.

Cogito, ergo sum

"The mark of the immature man is that he wants to die nobly for a cause, while the mark of the mature man is that he wants to live humbly for one." Mr. Antolini, quoting Wilhelm Stekel, to Holden Caulfield in, "The Catcher in the Rye"

"The unexamined life is not worth living." Socrates, quoted in Plato's *Apology*

About The Author

Once upon a time there was the merriest of monkeys happily cavorting in the jungle canopy. His name was Author. One day, brachiating with lithe, muscular movements, Author spied a favored fruit. Reaching from a weakened branch the branch broke and Author tumbled to the ground. Bruised and scratched Author knuckled himself from the ground and viewed his surroundings. Suddenly a panther appeared. Author rose and ran for the safety of a nearby pond. Swimming and reaching an islet he noticed silvery arrows all about and captured one with his freed hands. He examined the creature from head to tail and then gently placed it back into the water. Author don't like fish much.

The Author may currently be found racking pool balls at the Flamingo Bar, the Mt. Olympus for inspired pool players, or grilling hot dogs at the world famous Coney Island Grill in beautiful downtown St. Petersburg, Florida.